SUNSET ON

HIBS

THE PLOT TO
DESTROY HIBERNIAN

DAVID DUFF

WITH EWAN FLYNN

ARENA
SPORT

This edition first published in Great Britain in 2025 by

ARENA SPORT
An imprint of Birlinn Limited
West Newington House
10 Newington Road
Edinburgh
EH9 1QS

www.birlinn.co.uk

ISBN: 9781913759018
EBOOK ISBN: 9781788854740

Every effort has been made to trace copyright holders and obtain their permission for the use of copyright
material. The publisher apologises for any errors or omissions and would be grateful if notified of any
corrections that should be incorporated in future reprints or editions of this book.

British Library Cataloguing-in-Publication Data
A catalogue record for this book is available on request from the British Library.

Designed and typeset by Polaris Publishing, Edinburgh
www.polarispublishing.com

Printed and bound by MBM Print SCS Ltd, Glasgow

FSC
www.fsc.org

MIX
Paper | Supporting
responsible forestry
FSC® C117931

David Duff was Chairman of Hibernian at one of the most extraordinary times in the club's history. Beginning his career as a lawyer in the early 1980s, he was one of the highest profile boardroom figures in Scottish football. He has also published a semi-autobiographical novel, *Whole of the Moon*, about life in open prison in the 90s.

Ewan Flynn is a freelance football writer whose work has featured across the media. He is the author of two books: *We Are Sunday League* and *When the Year Ends in One: How Tottenham Hotspur's 1991 FA Cup Win Saved the Club and Transformed English Football.*

CONTENTS

Publisher's Note

This book was first submitted in 2021. As was good practice, text referring to Sir Tom Farmer was referred to his lawyers for review. The authors incorporated a number of comments made by Sir Tom's representatives while rebutting others. We resubmitted the text. The subsequent response made it clear that Sir Tom had no intention of allowing the text to print, one demand stating that he wished any reference to him excised. In the light of this, we had no option but to hold the text until after Sir Tom's death. We are aware of the controversy surrounding this time at Hibs but believe that David Duff has an absolute right to have his own story of those extraordinary years placed on record.

To my late grandmother, Nellie Fox of The Canongate,
and 'the goalie' Andy Goram

So with the Darkest Days behind
Our ship of Hope will steer
And when in doubt just keep in mind
Our motto – Persevere.

Leith Fisherman's prayer

FOREWORD

As I turned up early for the press conference at the Caledonian Hotel on a sunny June day back in 1990, Wallace Mercer looked a worried man.

The news had just broken about Hearts 'takeover' of Hibs, a story the *Edinburgh Evening News* would describe as the biggest to hit Edinburgh since World War II. This should have been Wallace's moment of triumph, but he didn't look a happy man. I tried to grab a quick word with him in the lobby, but he refused to speak to me – very unlike Wallace. Something had gone wrong.

It had been flagged up that David Duff would be there to formally hand over Hibs and all its assets to Hearts. But there was no sign of the Hibs chairman. Most press conferences are fairly mundane, but this one kicked off like a Hollywood movie with cameras flashing and a mob of reporters shouting questions. I managed to catch Wallace's eye. "Where is David Duff? Has he agreed to sell you his shares?" Wallace hesitated, looked right through me and moved on to another question. I repeated the question: "Has David Duff sold you his shares?" Again, a blank. This was a key point most seemed to be missing.

Mercer had just acquired a 66% majority of shares in Hibs from the mysterious Monaco-based tax-exile David Rowland and his allies. But he needed David Duff's 13.5% share to get over 75% to comply with the Takeover Code of the UK Companies Act and under Stock Exchange rules. Mercer and Rowland had thought Duff would just roll over and agree to sell when they ambushed him the day before with the deal.

As the press conference broke up, I rushed into the lobby to call the office and tell them it was not a done deal after all. David Duff had not sold his shares. Once he had recovered from the shock overnight, Duff had decided not to roll over. It's a position he resolutely stuck to in the days ahead despite intense pressure from Rowland, Mercer, the Bank of Scotland and the unlikeliest of other sources.

Looking back, it might have been better for him to take the money and run. He could have walked away that day with over £1 million. But he didn't, and for this alone he deserves the chance to have his say in the Hibs story.

When Ewan Flynn approached me about this book, I warned him to expect a legal onslaught, and I was right. Attempts 35 years on to block publication were ridiculous and a bit pathetic. It only reinforced my belief that David Duff had that right, especially after all he had been through. Unfortunately, many other players in the saga have died since then, notably Sir Tom Farmer and Wallace Mercer.

When I'd first met David Duff as new Hibs chairman in the late 80s, I found him a likeable guy, full of youthful exuberance – he was only 33 – and with big ambitions for Hibs. He was very much part of the City-slicker Zeitgeist of that era. However, I was a critic when he launched Hibs as a PLC listed on the

Stock Exchange. I didn't think it was the right fit for a club of Hibs' size and had serious misgivings about the mysterious Mr Rowland. Who was he and what was his interest in Hibs? But on that day at the Caledonian Hotel in June 1990 I recognised Duff had decided to do the right thing. However, he would never get any credit for it and would end up vilified and smeared in the media with his reputation ruined.

Many would say he brought it on himself, overreaching in his ambition and naïve trust – even conceit – that he could handle Rowland. It was his lack of judgment after all that had placed Hibs in a perilous, near fatal situation. Down the road a few years later he would be convicted for mortgage fraud, something separate from his life at Hibs. For many, if not most, this irretrievably damaged his reputation. But in all my dealings with David Duff over the years I found him to be truthful. Of all the main players in the 'takeover' saga he was the most open and transparent and at times seemed the only one genuinely interested in Hibs as a football club.

Ten years later I would track him down in London, long after he'd left Edinburgh. I was preparing a legal defence for a libel writ Sir Tom Farmer had served against me on reports about Hibs. I thought he might be too bruised and bitter by what he'd been through, but immediately he agreed to go on the record and offered to sign a sworn affidavit.

Today, many might prefer to dismiss his story out of hand. After all, it does not chime with the 'official mythology' and 'media narrative' that it was Sir Tom Farmer, and he alone, who 'saved' Hibs. But more open-minded readers should be prepared to look at the facts and weigh up the evidence that's available. David Duff is an open book on the subject, but Sir Tom and many others never were . . . as I was to find out.

No one can deny that the Kwik Fit and property tycoon played a key role bringing financial security and stability to a club in crisis when he stepped in as a guarantor with the Bank of Scotland. He was a phenomenal business success, worth hundreds of millions, and had a lot of clout not just with financial institutions, but also as one of Scotland's biggest media advertisers.

But overlooked in the 'official narrative' is that there were also others ready to step in and 'save' Hibs, notably the former club chairman Kenny Waugh and the Borders duo of David Elliot and Walter Allan of the Institute of Economic Affairs fame. No matter, the bank favoured Sir Tom.

Another aspect the 'official narrative' never got a handle on, but 'insiders' in Edinburgh's finance and property sector were all too well aware of, was that Wallace Mercer's 'takeover' was as much, if not more, about property than football. The media had already reported in the months prior to the takeover bid that jockeying had begun to build a new stadium out on the city bypass – Hearts at Millerhill, Hibs at Straiton, while David Murray, the Rangers chairman, was hovering around with his Hermiston site as an alternative for Hearts. And then there was the potential of Easter Road, 11 acres of land (stadium and the 'old car park') right next to the Lochend Butterfly which the council was opening up for commercial and residential development.

All in, there was big money to be made. David Duff was very open about this as he fought to stay on at Hibs and believed this double-whammy of a property deal could turbo-charge a Hibs challenge against the Glasgow duopoly. He also told me and others about a summons he'd had from Sir Tom to his house in Barnton. He had a startling proposal which Duff refused to accept, and this was the beginning of a very messy end to his time at Hibs.

Not long after I had my one and only sit-down interview with Sir Tom. I'd gone to his office at Roseburn with a colleague to talk about his plans for the future of Hibs. After some general questions – he kept addressing me as Mr Pia – I asked who was this 'Tom Harrison' he'd appointed to the Hibs board. Sir Tom was rather patronising in a reply along the lines of: "Mr Pia, you may not know this but in business you sometimes appoint people who are your friends." I said that may well be the case, "But is it not because he's your property developer and you want him to work on potential projects at Straiton and the Easter Road–Lochend Butterfly."

He exploded out of his seat, jabbing his finger in my face: "I dinnae like where you're coming from, son. I dinnae like where you're coming from." He then stormed out of the room. We sat where we were and waited as he paced up and down the hall. After a few minutes he came back in. I explained it was a reasonable question, very much in the public interest. Fans deserved to know why people were appearing out of nowhere as board members, especially after the experience with David Rowland. Sir Tom was struggling to regain control. The meeting was over. The next day I got a call from a Hibs director asking what I had done to Sir Tom? He'd gone "ballistic".

This set the tone for our future relationship, or rather lack of it. He refused any further interviews in the years ahead. But there would be an unusual denouement years later after our legal stand-off withered away.

One thing did jar when Sir Tom took full control of Hibs in 1991. The club was immediately separated from its main asset (the stadium and land), and Hibs had to start paying £75,000 annual rent to HFC Holdings, Sir Tom's parent company. He also announced Hibs would have the right to stay at Easter Road "for the foreseeable long-term future".

Fast forward six months to January 1992 and Hibs were on the front pages again, announcing plans to quit Easter Road after 100 years and move out to a site on the city bypass. This would be done with a new company, Straiton Ltd, of which Sir

Tom was a director with Tom Harrison as its managing director. After over a year there'd be a U-turn and Hibs would stay put at Easter Road, which would be redeveloped (the project took more than ten years to complete).

However, plans to move to Straiton were revived a decade later, in 2003, where Sir Tom and Tom Harrison were now active with a company called Morston Assets, described in the media as a "property firm owned by Kwik Fit tycoon Sir Tom Farmer and Norwich-based property entrepreneur Tom Harrison". Morston Assets had "£1.25 billion of projects under development and was responsible for bringing Ikea and Sainsbury to Straiton . . . where it owns 600,000sq ft". Hibs had also announced plans splashed on the front page of the *Evening News* in 2000 for a £35-million development at Easter Road next to the Lochend Butterfly as part of a consortium with none other than Morston Assets. But it was knocked back by Edinburgh Council, and two years later *The Scotsman* reported the old car park – "a hugely lucrative area of wasteland behind Easter Road stadium" – was now up for sale. A club spokesman was quoted: "The land placed on the market by the holding company is not required by the club."

Sir Tom's PR lackeys would often brief that I had an 'agenda' against Sir Tom. I did. It was for openness and transparency about what was going on at Easter Road. (He also had his agenda – to shut me up). I'd also only started reporting on the off-field activities and their negative impact on the football club in 1996, five years after Sir Tom had taken over. Insiders at Hibs had told me the debt was rising at an alarming rate. The original cost of the Famous Five Stand had risen from £4 million to £8 million, with Sir Tom getting directly involved, while Hibernian Hospitality Ltd, a new company set up for functions, turned into a fiasco and waste of money.

This was having a negative effect on the football club. Between 1996 and 2003 Hibs would go through nine managers and five chairmen with numerous directors toppled, among them Allan Munro, who had first got Sir Tom involved in Hibs. The club would also be relegated in 1998. Meanwhile, Hibs' debt would keep soaring to over £17 million 'officially' by 2003. This was during a decade when Hibs were regularly bringing in millions in transfer fees from the likes of Andy Goram, Ulises de la Cruz, Ulrik Laursen, Darren Jackson, Kenny Miller etc.

Throughout my reporting I always offered Sir Tom right of reply, and even on one occasion an 800-word column to give his side of the story, which he refused. Many people approached me with information but would then back off and not go on the record. An exception was Ian Blackford, then a rising star in finance and politics, and latterly the leader of the SNP at Westminster. Ian phoned me after I'd quoted him as a concerned fan. He'd had a call from his boss that Sir Tom, a major client, wanted Ian to retract his quote and say I'd made it up. Ian refused to do so but thought he should warn me. I appreciated his integrity and backbone as so many others seemed intimidated.

Sir Tom and I also ended up together in *Private Eye*. The satirical magazine ran a piece on how he'd gone through three different PR companies in as many months trying to shut down my reports. It concluded: "The saintly Sir Tom Farmer's latest PR outfit have been doing the rounds trying to dig up dirt on Pia. All, happily, to no avail." I could see the funny side, but that's not how it worked out for David Duff.

Sir Tom also liked to say there was no one else interested in Hibs, so he had to continue to shoulder the responsibility, despite the fact he repeated ad nauseam that he had no interest in football. I knew this was not the case, and that there were three Edinburgh businessmen – a financier, a car dealer and a publican – who had expressed interest. None of them would go on the record. One day, though, I got a call from Brian

Kennedy, the double-glazing tycoon, who I'd never met before. As he was asking me about the situation at Hibs I interrupted him: "I take it you're interested in buying Hibs?" Indeed, he was. I guessed he was in town to meet Sir Tom, so I staked out the Kwik Fit office with a photographer to see if we could catch them together on camera. Brian was unaware of this and when we published, he phoned. He had no problem about it going public but told me Sir Tom was not a happy man. However, the Hibs owner could no longer say there was "no one else out there".

During this period, 1997–99, Sir Tom sued on two occasions. Neither case ever went to court. I knew this would happen. Most libel writs don't – they're just frighteners to stop publication. But if it had, the media would have had a field day with all the high-profile characters involved, including of course Sir Tom. I must admit a part of me relished the prospect. Meantime, no apology, no retraction, no redaction, no correction was ever published. I don't know if there was ever any secret back-room deal to appease Sir Tom, but I was never privy to any.

The attitude of the football club board also changed towards me. Initially hostile, some directors started speaking off the record as they had been unaware of certain facts I'd revealed. Douglas Cromb, former club chairman, also had told me the board had never wanted to move from Easter Road in the first place. As for the football side, one manager pulled me aside to tell me to "keep up the good work". The scrutiny helped him put his case for more support for the football side of things at Easter Road.

Libel cases often turn into a war of attrition. They tend to be long, drawn out and so expensive that they are out of the reach of most mortals. One of the *Scotsman* lawyers pointed out to me both sides (the lawyers, that is) like to keep the meter running as long as possible. Then there are the internal tensions they create at media outlets. Nearly all media organisations, except for the BBC, are commercial enterprises, and some in management didn't appreciate the fact I was upsetting one of their biggest advertisers. Kwik Fit double-page ads were famous across national and local newspapers, while the 'Kwik Fit fitter' was one of the most recognisable jingles on television. I did recognise this, but asked the MD on one of the several occasions I was hauled into his office, what's a journalist supposed to do? Whose side are we on? The public's or corporate advertisers'? I got no answer to that. Throughout the whole process, journalist colleagues displayed a solidarity which I'll always appreciate, and their support created a further dilemma for the management.

But it got to the stage I felt I was bearing too much of the burden of defending the case and was being undermined from within. It came to a head when I had a stand-up row with one editor after I found out he'd met Sir Tom behind my back. (A couple of colleagues had tipped me off). The editor wanted me sacked, but other senior journalists had my back. However, I decided to leave, but less than a year later I was back in the building in a new role as *The Scotsman*'s diary columnist.

Colleagues had tipped off the National Union of Journalists about my situation. The union's magazine, *The Journalist*, decided to run a double-page spread – 'Dodgy Silencer' – about Sir Tom, me and *The Scotsman*. That, along with the *Private Eye* piece, put the issue in the public domain. To this day I don't know who tipped off *Private Eye* and *The Journalist*. I've always loved my trade and the people in it, making a lot of great friends. Whenever anyone has a pop at the media, I point out the problem is not the journalists but corporate owners and senior management. Ground-floor hacks, for all their quirks and flaws, are a breed apart.

As the legal battle exhausted itself, I'd run into Sir Tom in my new role every so often at public events. He didn't exactly try and befriend me but was keen to smooth things over between us and asked me on a couple of occasions to meet him for a coffee at the George Hotel. I turned him down both times, which he didn't like. But I did make a point of telling him it was a great pity he was never a real Hibs fan and was not interested in football. If so, with his drive, energy and financial power he'd have made sure Hibs were winners.

But that was David Duff's dream – to make Hibs winners. He had a plan, he had a passion. It never worked out and remains one of the great 'what ifs' in Hibs history. This is his story.

Simon Pia
Edinburgh
September 2025

PROLOGUE

"WHO'S THE ABSOLUTE worst person you can imagine to buy Hibernian?"

On Sunday, 3 June, 1990, I travelled down to London to find out the answer to this question at a meeting with the club's largest shareholder. He had made a secret deal to sell Hibs behind my back. I was 36 years old and had been chairman of Hibernian – the club I love – for three seasons. My world was about to fall apart.

*

This is a book I thought I would never write. It has taken over 30 painful years to reach a place in my life where I feel finally able to reveal what really happened before, during and after the bid to buy Hibernian Football Club by the then-chairman of Heart of Midlothian, Wallace Mercer.

The whole sorry episode was a destructive and unnecessary

attack on something cherished by its community. A community that I have proudly belonged to ever since becoming besotted with Hibs as a schoolboy.

I am aware that this book may reopen some old wounds. That is regrettable, but I do not believe the full truth has ever been told about the attempt to destroy Hibs and create an 'Edinburgh United'. The facts cannot remain a casualty of this affair for ever.

I am the only person who can tell this story. Whether I wanted to be or not, I was the central character in one of the most infamous chapters in Scottish football. I acknowledge that I made many mistakes. At times, I allowed my ego and ambition to cloud my judgement. I also accept that had I been wiser, stronger, and more humble, perhaps the story would have been different.

Whatever has been said since, it is a fact that but for my decision to refuse to sell my shares to Wallace Mercer, Hibs as we know them would no longer exist. This is the story of how I found myself in the position of being the person who had to decide which way the bid would end. I was the man responsible for determining whether Hibernian Football Club would live or perish.

I will try to explain in the following pages why I made the decisions that I did. I will also share my experiences during what was a critical period in the development of modern British football. As well as raising a smile and even the odd tear, I hope they serve as a cautionary tale. Football clubs are precious. Now, more than ever, we must protect them from those that do not have their best interests at heart.

This is not the story of those few individuals in Edinburgh's elite who caused dismay in the city and across Scottish football by pouncing upon a wounded Hibernian for their own selfish interests. This is my story. It is time to tell it.

*

The Scottish Cup Final – 2016

"When Hibs go up to lift the Scottish Cup, you'll be dead."

So sang rival fans on the terraces at Tynecastle Park and Ibrox whenever we visited. Hibs had not won the cup since 1902. On 21 May, 2016, those chants were silenced for ever. A unique occasion, where for the first time two teams from outside Scottish football's top tier contested the Scottish Cup final, saw Hibernian beat Rangers 3-2.

I'd aimed to bring this hoodoo to an end three decades earlier when I was chairman. We came close, taking Hibs to a Hampden semi-final in the 1988/89 season. I really thought that was going to be our year. But Celtic broke my heart on that April Sunday.

Leaving the national stadium that day, we would not have believed that it would take a further 27 years to capture the silverware. Our aim was to challenge for the top honours every season. Ironically, in the year the jinx was broken, Hibs were not a great team, having failed for the second successive campaign to gain promotion to the Premiership.

The question for all Hibs fans is: should it have taken nearly three decades, from that 1989 semi-final at Hampden Park, for the club to reach this milestone? Should the once-great Hibernian ever have been condemned to a third consecutive season in the Championship? Let me take you back to an era when Hibs knocked on the door of sustained success and explain how that door was slammed in our faces and by whom.

This is a remarkable tale of cross and double-cross when the sunshine on Leith was nearly extinguished by the black clouds of greed.

ONE

HARD TIMES AT THE HIBS

SUCCESS CAME TO me when I was very young. By the age of 31, having trained as a solicitor in a small London firm and got married, I moved to a country practice in Wiltshire. My personal client base consisted of property developers, businessmen, academics, and even future Oscar-winning actors. So strong was my business in the sleepy West Country that I was quickly able to expand, opening a London office on the Fulham Road.

Travelling between my offices, I acquired more high-profile clients, including the forerunner of the Portman Building Society and a significant part of the Saudi royal family. I had trained with a young woman who became a very close friend, and she agreed to run my London office. Jane Keeble was the daughter of Sir Curtis Keeble, who had been the British Ambassador to the USSR, and sister of Sally Keeble, who would become a junior minister in the Blair government.

I declined an offer to relocate to Saudi Arabia as a British business and legal adviser. I also turned down the chance of being Ken Culley's deputy at the West of England Building Society, although I remained their solicitor. Significantly, for future events, I was single-handedly responsible for completely re-writing their entire mortgage documentation. However, I was happiest in the capital and much more the London lawyer than the "solicitor from Wiltshire", as the press – in less-than-glowing terms – later came to describe me.

For a London legal practice in the 1980s, Christmas was a busy social time. We were Mrs Thatcher's yuppies. The opulent parties were endless. Hosts would try to outdo each other with the excellence of their food, the volume of drink they served and the grandeur of surroundings. Failure to receive an invitation to the best bashes would be considered a snub that was hard to recover from.

But the patronage did not come exclusively from the supposed upper echelons of society. Most of the big spenders who frequented the Fulham gatherings were rough diamonds who had started life as plumbers, plasterers, electricians and bricklayers. Their skills and their savvy allowed them to turn phenomenal profits – converting derelict houses, which they picked up for a song, into highly desirable London flats.

The veritable showroom of Rolls-Royces and Bentleys outside these events testified to their success. The sleek, two-tone Corniche, registration 456 DFD, was mine. Forgive my excess. I was young, I was cocky, and it was the mid-1980s. Many of the others belonged to my clients. Another West London solicitor, Sheila Rowland, moved in the same circles. She was the second partner in Mackworth Rowland – a practice located in fashionable Chelsea, just off the King's Road.

Sheila was by this time the first former wife of South London boy-done-good David Rowland. He'd grown up the son of a scrap-metal merchant to become the biggest of all the local property developers. Before their marriage ended, the Rowlands had two children, Jonathan and Venetia. Rowland was a private man who left London for Paris after doing his first big deal. None of the Fulham boys had ever met him. He was camera- and publicity-shy, ever since the *London Evening Standard* described him as a man with the "emotions of an ashtray".

Sheila and I often found ourselves on opposite sides of property transactions, as we acted for either of the developers. But we also shared mutual clients who would buy some properties through me and others with her. The Fulham set were a paranoid bunch, you see, and some would never trust just one firm to handle all their business dealings. One such mutual client was Melvyn Legge, who remains my friend to this day.

In December 1985, Melvyn informed me that Sheila's firm was having its own Christmas party. My friend (and client) Michael O'Leary was apparently on the guest list. Typically, my own neurosis kicked in. I was convinced that the invite was part of a plot to steal away one of my most active clients. I discovered that Michael had arranged to go to the party with Dick Hitchcock and Alan King, the local timber merchants who used both Sheila and me for legal work. All of the men were good friends. We belonged to a Friday club where we would meet at the end of each week for lunch which, amid a binge of arrogance and excess, often lasted until the wee hours.

Most of the Friday club were committed Masonic members. I had no wish to be part of that archaic nonsense. My experience of that clandestine world was limited to the odd trip to Brighton as an invitee on 'ladies' night'. These were the non-ceremonial dinners, where members could bring their wives and friends as a thank you for contributing to their success. I learned the hard way that they are not amused by outsiders rolling up a trouser leg. At these secretive celebrations, I heard hushed stories of drunken drivers avoiding arrest, evidence of criminal investigations and court summonses disappearing as if by magic. If you knew the handshake, planning permissions would be waved through. By contrast, the entire staff of Mackworth Rowland was female.

They had their own ways of attracting the Fulham boys.

It was easy for me to gatecrash the party and foil Sheila's plan. I joined Melvyn, Michael, Alan, Dick and their other cronies in a local pub. And having sunk a few pints of light and bitter, we proceeded to Rosalind Mackworth's Chelsea home to celebrate Christmas and toast the booming property market. If Sheila was surprised to see me, she hid it well. I was graciously welcomed through the front door. Melvyn and I climbed the stairs to a large drawing room filled with an eclectic mixture of people. We had been slow to pass through the threshold and could see that in front of the grand fireplace, Michael and Dick were already being entertained by the charming Mrs Mackworth. They were all very drunk. We turned left into an alcove where a small group of men were quaffing champagne, eating nuts and keeping very much to themselves.

With the confidence of the half-cut, I joined their conversation, asking on spec whether they were in the property game. A tall, bespectacled man – looking like he'd been sent by central casting to play the role of 'stereotypical accountant 1' – introduced himself as Jeremy James. He explained that he was the managing director of a company called INOCO. He was clearly the sidekick. The man stood next to him – casually dressed, short and bearing the well-nourished look of one of Mrs Thatcher's movers and shakers – was the star. It was difficult to see his face, which was shrouded by the expensive, seductive smoke of the Romeo y Julieta cigar held in his right hand. Eventually, through the haze a thickly bearded profile, topped with a mop of brown hair, came into focus. He referred to himself simply as David.

Soon the penny dropped. This was the mysterious 40-something entrepreneur and former husband of Sheila, David Rowland. The conversation was quickly reversed. Rowland was now grilling me with questions about my practice. He then enquired straight out: what percentage of value did I charge for conveyancing? And could I competently deal with commercial transactions? He was interested in the size of my firm, my energy and my hunger. I was all too eager to please.

Rowland told me that he might have some work to send my way. He explained that he dealt in commercial property and then further quizzed me on my experience and knowledge. He took my card. It contained one of the first mobile phone numbers in the United Kingdom, when Vodafone was a baby company, making enormous, heavy, brick-sized handsets for yuppies like me.

Suddenly, there was a commotion over at the fireplace. Michael O'Leary had been fiddling with an ornate figure of a horse, which apparently was a valuable piece of china. "Please be careful," said Rosalind anxiously, "it's Ming." At that point, Michael unwittingly broke off a hind leg, much to the distress of our host. "Don't worry," said Michael, "I'll buy you a new one." The group by the fireplace were beckoning Melvyn and I to join them, but David quickly suggested we should move on. Mr Mackworth was getting angry on his wife's behalf. He had started to corral the most inebriated guests into two taxis.

Melvyn and I picked up Sheila and her daughter Venetia, who had been downstairs in the kitchen chatting. I was staggered by the control David exerted over those around him. At the click of his fingers, his ex-wife left her legal partner's party to follow him. The rest of us were in tow, with no idea where we were headed. I had been used to going to fancy places in town, and I assumed we would be off to a known haunt. However, our taxi drew up in Berkeley Square, and we were tipped out in front of the world-renowned Annabel's. The club was a members' only establishment, virtually impossible to join unless you moved in influential circles. I had never been there before. David Rowland was well known here. The owner immediately greeted him with a hug and we were escorted to a table in the restaurant. I danced with Venetia. She was a shy young woman of about 19, not the typically entitled trust-fund child I'd imagined. After we all said goodnight, I never expected to see or hear from David Rowland again.

At this time, I lived in the rural town of Marlborough. I was a partner in a successful law firm that was expanding to have offices in four locations. I had big houses, racehorses and drove the car of my choice. It was intoxicating. I was living proof of the Thatcherite dream, or so I thought, but I was still full of ambition. It was all such a long way from my working-class upbringing in Scotland.

On my 32nd birthday on 17 February, 1986, I was overseeing a case at the West London Magistrates' Court. My family were waiting for me to come back to Wiltshire to celebrate my big day. As I left court, I took a call on my smart Vodafone. It was David Rowland. He wanted me to come to his Mayfair office without delay. He needed to instruct a solicitor that very day. I dropped my birthday celebrations and headed to where I had been summoned. Rowland asked me to act on his behalf in the acquisition of 19 large office buildings worth many millions of pounds. It was the biggest, potentially most profitable, piece of work that had ever come my way. I became one of just a handful of solicitors entrusted by Rowland to carry out his affairs. The others all worked for massive city firms, which today form the 'Magic Circle' of London lawyers.

Over the summer, I spent 14 hours a day looking at titles, leases, tenancies and raising multiple questions and observations. These properties were going through a Dutch nominee and into a listed corporation called INOCO, for which I now acted. Upon completion, 19 lawyers sat on one side of a long table. Each of the solicitors was dealing with just one of the vast properties in the deal. On the opposite side of the table sat Darren – my articled clerk – myself and 17 empty seats. It was comical. But Rowland was impressed with my work. I had done what he wanted, and our relationship ramped up.

*

Even though my life increasingly revolved around London and the West Country, I would still try to get up to Edinburgh as often as possible. I loved my hometown. I still do. The early part of my childhood was spent in the city, and it was my cousin Stewart who had first taken me to Easter Road. These were the days of massive rolling terraces, and I remember being deposited on top of a wall so that I could get a view of the pitch. I must have been seven or eight years old. Even now, more than 60 years on, I can still smell the deliciously awful food, the newly printed match programmes, the Woodbine smoke and the alcohol-breath of fans. These were as much a part of an afternoon or evening watching Hibs as the football.

My wife's parents lived in Auld Reekie, and we frequently went to see them. I struck up a close friendship with my brother-in-law, Jim Gray, who, like me, was a lifelong Hibee. Jim and I would regularly take a seat in Easter Road's main stand to watch the Hibs. The stadium was dilapidated, the team without inspiration and the crowds sparse. Only the hardy remained, watching the once-famous green jerseys toiling year in year out to avoid relegation. Hibernian was wallowing in mediocrity.

The massive terracing of my youth had gone, replaced with a small, low-quality stand. Behind it sat six acres of land, ripe for a potential city-centre development. The chairman was Edinburgh bookie, Kenny Waugh. His board consisted of men like him who no doubt cared deeply but lacked any plan to lift Hibs from the doldrums. Alex Miller would be appointed the club's new manager four months into the 1986/87 season.

A few weeks before his arrival, Hibs played out a particularly unattractive game at home to St Mirren, losing 0-1 on 13 September, 1986. Sitting in the stand, I casually asked, "Can this club be bought?" I was with Jim and some of his pals, and my throwaway comment was picked up by one of them who said, "I know a member of the board." It was a simple statement that would change my life irrevocably. On a whim, he agreed he would approach the director in question on my behalf to see if we could find a way in for me to meet Kenny Waugh.

In no time, I was sitting down for a chat with that director, Alan Young, and during our meeting in a local pub, he told me that Kenny Waugh wanted out of Hibs. He even confided what Kenny would take for his shares. Compared to the eye-watering amounts that clubs change hands for today, £800,000 seems a snip. But in the mid-1980s, this was a tidy sum for a business that lost money season after season. Back then, Hibs had a local double-glazing firm sponsoring their shirt. Corporate hospitality was unheard of. And the average home gate barely even covered the players' wages.

Tottenham Hotspur chairman Irving Scholar, like me in his 30s and prospering in the London property game, provided a roadmap. He had become the first person to float a football club on the London stock exchange. Scholar played a pivotal role in increasing the television revenue the top English clubs received from broadcasters. He would also redefine the British transfer market by negotiating the sale of Chris Waddle to Marseille for a whopping £4.5 million in 1989. It was the third-highest sum ever paid for a footballer at the time. Scholar was an innovator, and my ideas seemed to fit his model. I believed that to compete with the best, the club needed a consistent, alternative and secure income. Furthermore, if we could float the club, fans too through the purchase of shares would have the chance to own a part of Hibernian. It seemed like a win-win.

The football industry was totally undervalued in the 1980s. Crumbling Victorian grounds and the scourge of hooliganism saw to that. As a blistering *Sunday Times* editorial from the middle of the decade put it, "A slum sport, played in slum stadiums, and increasingly watched by slum people." Most clubs still belonged to local businessmen. Like Kenny Waugh, they were usually self-made. They saw buying their hometown team as a way of enhancing their standing in the local community or did it out of a sense of civic pride. Often both. It was clear to me that the professional game was nowhere near to realising its full business potential. Things were, however, ripe for change.

I had the money needed to buy Hibernian. But to realise my ambition of restoring the club to its former glories, I needed a big loan or, better still, a partner. While I was pursuing a meeting with Kenny Waugh, I went to Sheila Rowland and asked her if David would be interested in buying Hibs with me. I explained my vision for the club and that I needed the backing of someone with a pedigree of experience on the stock exchange. David Rowland, with his apparent Midas touch in business, absolutely fitted the bill. The very next day, Sheila confirmed David was willing to be convinced, so I went to meet him determined to sell him my dream. He did not require much persuading. In total, with costs, we needed £900,000. The deal we thrashed out was that I would put up £100,000, while he invested £300,000. Rowland would then also lend the venture the £500,000 balance.

In exchange for this line of credit, I would buy all the shares and give him an option to purchase 60% for £1. Rowland would use all his expertise and contacts book to help me float Hibernian on the stock exchange. After that, he promised to source property assets that would underpin the newly formed company. Sheila would also be joining the board.

The negotiations were completed in David Rowland's swanky house in Elizabeth Street, Belgravia. Rowland offered me a cigar and, as we smoked Cuba's finest, he leant over and, in his cockney accent, simply said: "All right. Let's shake on our deal."

With Hibs ending the 1986/87 season dismally, winning just two games of the last 11 to finish fourth from bottom in the Premier Division, Kenny Waugh, at last, agreed to meet. My fantasy was becoming a reality. I left Rowland's home fully confident that I would be the next chairman and owner of

Hibernian Football Club. It was an incredible feeling for a lad who had attended Edinburgh's Trinity Academy as a teenager and followed Hibs home and away with his schoolmates. Back then, I belonged to the Carlton branch of the Hibernian Supporters' Club. I would sell bingo cards for the youth team, securing free travel to away matches on the Carlton coach. I was a true fan, emotionally invested in the club. By acquiring Hibs, I believed I could make us the best team in Scotland and restore the club to where it belonged, playing European football year in, year out. The businessman would not always sit comfortably alongside the boy fan inside me. But I was convinced that a great company would create a winning team.

Dealing with Kenny Waugh proved a long, laboured and difficult task. In truth, he was conflicted. Kenny was still fond of the prestige that came with being chairman but increasingly found the responsibilities of the position wearisome. I suppose, in village-like Edinburgh, it was inevitable that the negotiations between us would be made public. One day I flew into Scotland to find Jim White from STV and a television crew waiting for me. I gave my first of many interviews at the airport.

I was desperate to finish the deal before the 1987/88 football season kicked off. I had sat with Jim Gray in the directors' box at the end of the previous campaign as Kenny's guest, but nobody then had been interested in who we were. My interview with Jim White changed that, and speculation was rife that I was the frontman for someone else. Rod Stewart's name was often touted. This despite his staunch support of Celtic precluding him from buying a rival club. Jim Kean at the *Daily Record* and Stewart Brown at the Edinburgh *Evening News* were also keen to know more about me. I spoke with them many times after the STV interview. There seemed to be widespread disbelief that, at my tender age, I could be doing this for myself. However, after they did some digging and found my name in the Carlton Hibs records, they accepted that I genuinely was a fan on a mission.

The negotiations moved to the Isle of Man. Hibs had agreed to play a pre-season tournament with a couple of English sides. So, as well as meeting with Kenny and the board, Jim Gray and I took in some football, sitting on the tiny stone terracing, in the summer sun while watching my prospective team.

The manager, Alex Miller, obviously knew who we were but kept a distance. His assistant, Peter Cormack, was much more friendly. Peter had been one of my heroes in the 1960s and, when he left Hibs, had a magnificent career playing for Nottingham Forest and Liverpool. Having served under Bill Shankly at Anfield, and the great Jock Stein with Scotland, Peter Cormack was a bona-fide legend in my eyes. Alex and Peter must have tipped the Hibs players off about the significance of our presence. They began giving us sly looks and, as footballers do, even aimed the odd bit of friendly banter our way. The fact Jim Gray and I looked pretty similar, sporting thick dark moustaches, gave them plenty of ammunition.

The Isle of Man trip proved decisive, and following further friendlies in the north of England, I cemented the deal. At a press conference in the Easter Road boardroom on 24 August, 1987, Kenny and I sat down and signed on the dotted line. I was now the owner and new chairman of Hibernian Football Club. Kenny stayed on as a director for a further year until we unhappily and permanently parted ways.

I immediately appointed Jim Gray as full-time managing director. As well as Sheila, David Rowland insisted on installing his faithful INOCO lieutenant, Jeremy James, on the club's board. Sheila became the first female director in Scottish football. From day one we would challenge the old conservative order in the Scottish game. This presented a challenge to some of our more 'traditional' rivals. On our first visit to Tynecastle, Wallace Mercer refused to allow a woman into the directors' room. Sheila was banished with the players and directors' wives to the players' lounge for the Edinburgh derby. She had a thoroughly miserable time and was not impressed with this overt sexism.

I protested in the week after the match, saying we, the directors of Hibernian, would boycott the next game unless all our board members were treated equally and with respect. Sure enough, Sheila's second visit to Tynecastle Park saw her break down barriers in the Hearts boardroom. How times change; in Ann Budge, Hearts have been led by a woman since 2014.

Based on their reputation, I expected similar problems when Sheila visited Ibrox for the first time the following season. Rangers had a small directors' room that was strictly for board members only. Beyond cleaning and catering staff, I understood that no woman had set foot in this room for over a century. Another bastion of male chauvinism was about to be shaken. When confronted with this challenge to the established 'etiquette', Rangers showed much more grace than our Edinburgh neighbours had managed. Their charming club secretary Campbell Ogilvie personally escorted the female English solicitor to meet smiling chairman David Murray.

Our manager, Alex Miller, had made his name at Ibrox, where he played as a defender under Jock Wallace. Famously Rangers' pre-season in those days required the players to run up 'Murder Hill' – the sand dunes at Gullane Beach – until they were sick or needed oxygen. I think this left a big impression on Alex when he embarked on his coaching career. He was more about graft than artistry. As a player, he would supplement his income by selling ice cream from a van he'd fitted with a chime to alert customers. Some punters would be shocked to find they were being served their scoop of chocolate or vanilla by the very same man they'd just witnessed marshal the Rangers backline.

Alex Miller's prodigious work ethic was there for all to see. He also proved to be highly innovative and was in the vanguard of those trying to implement sports science into the sceptically insular world of Scottish football. But my initial impressions of him when we met were that he was a dour Glaswegian, distant from his players and lacking any real sense of humour. Looking back now, I dread to think what he must have made of me. What Alex did possess was a wish list of transfer targets which he quickly gave me. There, on the list, was Neil Orr. As a regular visitor to Upton Park, West Ham being my adopted team down south, I knew the player well and encouraged Alex to sign him. Technically, Orr joined Hibs on the same date I bought the club. And he made his debut the very next day, even managing a goal in our League Cup tie against Queen of the South.

On the day Kenny Waugh and I had actually agreed and initialled terms, we were playing Rangers in our first home game of the season. It was an evening game under the lights. I took my seat in the Easter Road directors' box as virtual chairman. Behind me sat Rangers player-manager – and Scottish football legend – Graeme Souness. Having been sent off on his Rangers debut against us the season before – sparking a mass brawl – perhaps wisely, he had decided not to select himself to play. What a night that was. Hibs scrapped to a superb 1-0 win against the champions – John Collins scoring the winner.

There would be difficult evenings ahead, but this was one to savour. Before the game, Alex had told me that, at the final whistle, I should go down to the Rangers dressing room and knock on the door. I was to poke my head in and say, "well done" if they won, "hard lines" if we won, and simply "good game" if it was a draw. I stole downstairs after the game, knocking gently below the sign that read 'Visitors'. As the door eased open, there in the middle of the room was Chris Woods, surrounded by his thoroughly dejected teammates. Securely held in the England goalkeeper's big hands were a vast tray of savoury mince pies and a massive teapot.

I took a deep breath, preparing to offer my words of condolence when suddenly I was bundled aside by an irate Mr Souness. The Rangers manager then proceeded to boot the tray out of Chris Woods' hands with a fierce punt. The teapot toppled as millions of pounds worth of humanity dived for cover. The pies went flying in the air. Some stuck to the ceiling. I quietly withdrew, closed the door and went to the home dressing room, where the mood was very different. Our players were buzzing. They were naked to a man, dancing, singing and joking. I recounted my experience in the Rangers dressing room, innocently asking whether I should complain about the mess Souness had made. "Chairman," Alex said, "let's hope he's kicking fucking pies every time he comes here." It brought the bloody house down.

TWO

THE ORANGE JUICE KID, BIG SAFE HANDS AND WEE MICKEY

FOR TOO LONG, Hibs had sold their best players. Our gem, John Collins, was reaching the end of his contract. And, according to the press, it was inevitable he would be moving on to a "bigger and better club". Not if I could help it.

One of the top agents of the day in Scotland was Bill McMurdo. His home was named "Ibrox" and was painted in red, white and blue, so it was not difficult to work out where his loyalties lay. He was, however, totally professional and did not bring his love of Rangers to the business table. Despite this, he was persona non grata at some clubs. One in particular – no prizes for guessing which – even banned him from their ground for a while. I always found him easy to deal with. He wanted what was best for his client but knew the market rate and did not make impossible demands. This was just as well as he was John Collins' agent.

In the days before freedom of contract, the clubs had complete control of players' rights. At the end of a contract, they could either re-sign or be sold on. It was often more attractive for clubs to cash in on a star rather than effectively 're-sign' him to a new contract. To keep a top player, you would need to rustle up a one-off six-figure 'loyalty' bonus to go alongside their improved weekly wage. In all football transactions, demand puts up the price. As John's contract came to an end, at least four clubs were willing to pay £800,000 for his services. In the late 1980s, that represented the top end of the market for a player. If we could hang on to John, I thought it would be a statement of intent to our rivals. A challenge to the established hierarchy of Scottish football.

John was known as 'the orange juice kid' as he didn't drink alcohol. His only vice, as far as I could tell, was a love of sunbeds. Fans who bought a match programme in the late 80s will remember John's bronzed face smiling back at them in an advert for the Electric Beach tanning studio on Lothian Road. John was the only Scottish professional footballer to have a suntan throughout the entirety of the Edinburgh winter.

John was the model professional. An enormously talented footballer. With such a sweet left foot, he was bound to attract interest from the best. As the players were close to my own age, I thought it prudent to leave their contract negotiations to Jim Gray and Alex. Jim was a top negotiator, able to put aside his fondness for talented footballers more easily than I was. On this occasion, however, I was able to give Jim a slight helping hand. I had cultivated an important secret relationship giving me the inside track on what our players were thinking about their futures. Stevie, the hairdresser, worked from his home in Easter Road.

Many of the players used Stevie because they could relax in private and I became a client too. He was happy to pass on stories about the players that few other chairmen would hear. Through Stevie, I knew before contract negotiations started that John Collins wanted to stay at Easter Road and what terms he would accept. Pound for pound, it was the best value haircut I've ever had.

The decision to try to re-sign John was taken and the matter was left to Jim to thrash out with Bill McMurdo. Happily, Bill thought that John's development would benefit from another three years at

Hibs. It was a real fillip when John agreed to sign a new contract, but we asked him to keep it under wraps for a week or two so that we could announce it on the back of our business plans. We wanted to make people sit up at the 'new Hibs'.

The secret did not leak. Within days of re-signing John, I was in my Fulham office going over some files when a call came through from the secretary of Ken Bates. Ken was the chairman of Chelsea Football Club, situated about a mile down the road from my London office. Ken invited me to Stamford Bridge for lunch that very day. I was intrigued enough to accept.

Nowadays, there would be no shortage of overpriced places to dine around Stamford Bridge. But back then, the best option was the directors' box overlooking the sunlit pitch. We chatted for about half an hour over smoked salmon sandwiches and Chablis before Ken said: "Well, you know why I asked you here. Can we talk about the boy Collins?"

I explained we were in the market to buy players, not sell them. Bates then suggested a player plus money deal. "How about our forward Roy Wegerle and cash?" Wegerle would have been a great addition to Hibs and was apparently open to playing in Scotland. He had played 14 first-team games for Chelsea, and one more would trigger a further payment to a former club. Ken was keen to offload him before then. Again, I repeated that John was not for sale. Next, he offered Pat Nevin in part exchange. Pat was a super talent at the top of his career. But Pat – and his independent thinking – didn't come without challenge for Chelsea.

I later heard a brilliant story where after bursting into the first team at Stamford Bridge, Pat was negotiating a new contract. The winger wanted parity with his teammates but felt he was being lowballed. During a meeting with Pat, Ken made the fatal mistake of leaving his office to attend to some other business. Quick as a flash, Pat rifled through a filing cabinet, perused the other players' contracts and worked out the exact average salary of a first-teamer. The chairman had no choice but to agree.

When I knocked Bates back again over John Collins after he'd tried to sweeten the deal a final time, he gave up. I returned to my office shaking my head. John Collins was going nowhere. But I'd just had a lesson in the in-your-face way football business 1980s-style was conducted. I did keep in touch with Ken, though. I always found him an entertaining character who was generous with his time and advice. He was interested in the Scottish game and would always go to Hampden to watch the cup final. I think he fancied Hibs as a feeder club for Chelsea. My ambition was far greater.

As for John Collins, he got his bumper re-signing fee and became our best-paid player. A local car dealer gave him an Audi to drive. He was content. His performances over the next season would see him named the 1987/88 Scottish Professional Footballers' Association Young Player of the Year. A true Hibs hero.

The whole team was lifted by John staying. Confidence is built on belief, and I felt the players were beginning to buy into the Hibs mission. Away from the pitch, we were making significant signings too. I brought Jimmy Kerr on to the board. He had been one of the Hibs goalies during the years of the 'Famous Five', and I wanted to make that link with the club's glorious past. He was a lovely man and enjoyed being a boardroom ambassador. He had worked with a previous chairman, Tom Hart, and had a real passion for the club.

We appointed Raymond Sparkes as commercial manager; he had previously worked at the club and boasted a deep understanding of the game's expanding business side. He was a great asset and full of innovative ideas that challenged the conventional wisdom in football. He convinced us to change the standard pocket-sized programme into a glossy matchday magazine. Inside, along with the obligatory club propaganda, fans could now find colour pictures as well as stories and opinions they might actually want to read.

One of Raymond's biggest coups was to negotiate a new jersey deal with sportswear superpower Adidas. There were stacks of kit arriving all the time, which he had to store in boxes along his office wall. Adidas sent Alex, Peter, Jim, Raymond and I quilted coats. We must have looked like a gang of Michelin men when we turned up to mid-winter matches identically dressed. John Collins would end up wearing Adidas boots for most of his career. For those of you who are into your football boots, I believe John became the first player in the world to score a goal in their new 'Predator' design when he was at Celtic. I'm sure most Hibs fans will agree with me that those Adidas Hibs strips are among the very best in the club's history.

With Raymond's help, I implemented a super-executive club, aimed at our most affluent supporters. They could enjoy a four-course meal, have players visit them after the game and select the 'Man of the Match'. One challenge we faced in offering this nascent football hospitality was that alcohol could not be sold inside Scottish football grounds. Raymond devised a cunning solution to this problem – we opened a free bar to our super-exec club members who, perhaps not by coincidence, became firm friends. Eventually, on the back of this success, we built corporate boxes behind glass. All of these things are old hat now, but then, they were cutting edge. We would be the club to imitate, producing different packages for every kind of Hibs supporter.

I made a point of going over to our fans before away games to applaud them. All teams do this now, but I believe I was a bit of a pioneer in showing simple appreciation for our supporters. To be honest, it wasn't always much fun. At Tynecastle, I would have to walk past the Hearts faithful, who loved to sing gleefully that I was guilty of sexual self-gratification. At least when I reached the sea of green in the away end, I'd get to hear the odd chant of "There's only one Davie Duff." Occasionally, at Easter Road, I would stand in the terraces and watch the game from there, green blazer and all. I wanted everyone to belong.

My first Edinburgh derby as chairman ended in a narrow defeat. Our goalkeeper was Alan Rough, the former Scotland number 1, and I remember having a chat with him as we sat in the stand on my second day at the club. Roughie was very personable, and it's no surprise he became a top broadcaster. I always liked him. Alex Miller was less keen. During the derby, Rough went walkabout and cost us the decisive goal. At fulltime, Alex said to me, "Chairman, we need a new goalkeeper. He will get us relegated." Roughie's days were numbered.

Football clubs have many elaborate systems for the recruitment of new players. There are the talent spotters who watch every junior match. You have the school sports masters (from Catholic schools during my time at Hibs) who recommend promising boys. There are the senior scouts who hear whispers about which established players might be available for transfer. There is even a handbook for managers listing every registered player in the country. And then, of course, there are the agents.

The bigger the club, the bigger the recruitment network. When it came to finding new stars at Easter Road, we were blessed with a secret weapon. Martin Ferguson, our avuncular reserve team manager, knew his football inside out. He also had a very famous sibling. Martin's brother, Alex, was the manager of one of the biggest clubs in the world, Manchester United. On several occasions when we needed a player, we would tap into the United network. Martin would ask Alex for a steer on players that could do a job.

However, at this early point, when Alex Miller's priority was a new goalkeeper, not even the Ferguson Connection could come up with a potential name. We soon heard from elsewhere that there was a fine keeper available and that for around £300,000, we could bring him to Hibs. Ian Andrews played for Leicester City and had made well over 100 appearances for the Foxes. Before signing the tall, agile, young goalie, we invited him up for a trial match with the first team. We watched on in horror as he had an absolute shocker. Peter Cormack quickly dubbed him Dracula (as he wouldn't come out of his goal if there was a cross). It became abundantly clear he was not the goalkeeper for us. We were all amazed subsequently when Andrews was signed by Celtic. Suffice to say, he couldn't fill Pat Bonner's gloves, making fewer than 10 appearances for the Bhoys before returning south.

Meanwhile, at Oldham Athletic, the legendary Joe Royle was in charge. He, too, had a goalkeeping dilemma. His problem was that he had a young shot-stopper who was proving a handful off the pitch. Returning from an away game on the Oldham team bus, this keeper had thrown a bottle that struck one of the coaching staff. It was a stupid act born out of youthful exuberance rather than malice. But Joe decided the boy needed to be moved on. By happy coincidence, this young man from Lancashire was the son of a former Hibs goalie.

I'll never forget the first time I met Andy Goram. He came up to Edinburgh on the train with the Oldham manager. Joe knew that Andy didn't have an agent and wanted to ensure his player received the best possible contract from us – an absolute class act.

Andy was small for his position. He was stocky (some away fans used a different word) and did not pass the eyeball test of what a top professional goalkeeper should look like. Within minutes of watching him play for the first time, however, I could see that he had springs in his legs and the most phenomenal hand-eye coordination. Andy could seemingly see things coming before they were even on their way. His extraordinary talent and single-minded determination would never come into question at

Easter Road. Andy certainly had a 'Georgie Best twinkle' in his eye and fed on fans' adoration. I think that was essential fuel for his performances.

He became our new number 1 in October 1987 for a club record fee of £325,000, quickly establishing himself as the best goalkeeper in Scotland. His kindness off the pitch would prove just as inspirational as his reflexes on it.

*

I always had mixed feelings on the days we had to go to Ibrox. On the one hand, it was a big game where I could feel my body literally throbbing with excitement and anticipation. On the other, I could expect some severe abuse from the Rangers supporters. Even sitting in the directors' box, I would be the target of insults from fans on all sides of my exposed seat. On one occasion, I was spat at. Some of the abuse, mostly that which name-checked the Pope or 'Fenian Scum', was beyond my comprehension.

For the uninitiated, I should explain our club's history. By tradition Hibs are Edinburgh's 'Catholic team', with a similar origin story to Celtic in Glasgow. During the potato famine of the 19th century, tens of thousands of Irish families settled in Scotland after fleeing starvation. The Hibernian Football Club was created in 1875 when the young immigrant men were denied access to football and sports clubs, reserved exclusively for 'traditional' Scotsmen. Hibernia was the Roman name for Ireland. Edinburgh-born James Connolly, a leading figure in the Irish Republican Movement and committed socialist, had been one of the club's early fans. For some time, Hibs' roots were used as cause to exclude the club from the Scottish Football League. Those bigoted fans who aimed their bile at us seemed to wish for a return to those dark days. The irony was that I was raised in a Protestant family and spent many of my teenage years in Bromley, Kent. I was yet to fully appreciate the real horrors of sectarianism.

I should say at this point that, unlike the Ibrox crowd, the Rangers directors were always hospitable, well-mannered and welcoming when we visited. At the end of the game, the directors of both clubs would share a wee dram in the boardroom. The players, once dressed, would come out to their own lounge and enjoy a drink with wives, girlfriends and match sponsors.

It was not difficult to recognise our party as directors, management and players were all dressed in green jackets, sporting the club badge on the breast pocket. Grey trousers were topped off with a white shirt and club tie. We were Hibernian Football Club.

While the players, adrenaline still pumping, could often be the source of trouble during these post-match formalities, there were occasions when they showed extraordinary kindness and grace. Despite often being the principal mischief-maker at the club, these were qualities that radiated from Andy Goram.

On this day, having had one drink and half an hour of post-match socialising, the players and club officials headed for the coach in small groups. Andy was usually the last to board, squeezing out every drop of the hospitality on offer. The coach was parked immediately outside the stadium in a space that would allow it to turn without impeding passing traffic. This meant the walk from the security of the grand entrance hall to the coach was only the width of the pavement. Not that this prevented a handful of Rangers supporters proffering their opinions upon modern-day Catholicism while questioning the legitimacy of our players' family lineage. Most of the visiting party made a quick dash for it. But not Andy.

The seats at the front of the coach would always be occupied by Alex Miller, Peter Cormack, Jim Gray and myself. Just like schoolboys, the players would pass by us, jostling for the prized seats at the very back. From my berth behind the driver, I could see Andy signing autographs for the young fans. He laughed off the abuse aimed at him from Rangers supporters. Within a couple of years, they would be hailing him a hero. As he boarded the bus, Alex Miller asked him where the last stragglers from the players' lounge were. Andy confirmed they were not far behind, before going to the very back of the bus in search of his favourite spot.

Across the road, an unseen voice shouted a name, and one of the Rangers fans, a wee laddie of eight or nine, turned around in response. The boy was adorned in Rangers colours, top to tail, with a bobble hat and scarf. The club crest covered his heart. It was a cold, clear afternoon. Dusk was approaching, but it was still light enough to see outside. Responding to the call, suddenly the boy took off running right in front of the coach. As he did so, a car was passing the coach travelling at about 30 miles an hour.

There was nothing the driver could do as the little boy ran straight into the road. The impact sent him spiralling into the air. He hit the ground right in front of the parked bus. Those of us looking out of the front window saw the whole thing, almost as if it occurred in slow motion. We sat frozen in our seats. It was a sickening sight. There was a stunned silence as the car came to a halt. The shocked driver stayed inside, switching off his engine before slumping forward, his head resting on the steering wheel. He was alone. Even the handful of fans closest to the boy's prone body failed to react.

Then, from the back of the coach, sprinting down the aisle as if to intercept a ball in his penalty area, came Andy Goram. He jumped down and was the first person to reach the injured boy. It was hard to comprehend how he had even seen the incident, let alone given such a rapid response. But there, through the front window, I witnessed the touching sight of a Scottish international clad in a green blazer, cradling the head of the child covered in Rangers blue. The absurdity of sectarianism was laid bare by an immense act of care and humanity.

I am pleased to say that we later discovered that the boy survived and made a full recovery. I often wondered, in the years when Andy thrilled the Ibrox crowd, did the wee boy talk of the time his broken body was cradled by his hero? It was not the only time the man showed such compassion.

When an idiotic fan in a Celtic shirt decided to throw a CS gas canister into the Hibs faithful during a match at Easter Road, the game was halted. Several people were severely affected by the tear gas. Even more were hurt in the ensuing crush, as fans tried desperately to escape.

I will never forget the sheer horror I witnessed while downstairs in the tunnel, seeing person after person escorted to the safety of the dressing room. Their streaming eyes just one symptom of the great distress they experienced that day. I thought a catastrophe was unfolding before me, and I was terrified. Fortunately, the effect of the gas passed quickly, and my initial fear that there would be fatalities began to recede. There were, however, 45 people who had been rushed to hospital. Some of them had sustained crush injuries in the initial panic.

We managed to finish the match. We lost, but the result was an irrelevance. Once the Celtic official party left (they did not stay long that day), we debriefed with the police and dealt with the press. The following day's front and back pages were dominated by this awful story. The perpetrator was later identified using enhanced CCTV. He had acquired the gas from a soldier in Germany.

As a board, we decided that Jim and I should visit those fans admitted to hospital. One of the casualties was a small boy. When we approached his bed, we saw that he already had a visitor in the shape of the Scotland goalkeeper. Immediately after the game, upon hearing that people had been hospitalised, Andy, without any prompting, had gone to visit the injured fans.

Andy Goram was not the tallest goalkeeper ever to appear between the sticks. But he had huge hands. And an even bigger heart.

*

Along with Andy and John Collins, I assumed Mickey Weir would be an integral player in the new successful team I wanted Alex Miller to build. Mickey was small in stature, but could run like a whippet and get crowds on their feet.

The wee man came from a large, working-class, Hibs-mad family, growing up in a one-bedroom flat in Granton in the north of Edinburgh, where he loved flying pigeons. He joined the club as an apprentice while working as a dishwasher in a hotel kitchen and playing amateur football for Portobello Thistle. In the time-honoured tradition, his first days at Easter Road were spent sweeping out the stands and cleaning the senior pros' boots. After the great Pat Stanton gave him his chance in the first team, Mickey's bravery on the ball quickly made him a fans' favourite. He was one of their own, and they loved him for it.

However, it was clear early on in my first season as chairman that our manager had become less than enamoured with the winger. In his attempts to modernise, Alex requested the club employ a dietitian. All the players were given personalised meal plans to follow. Before a game, the team and officials would meet at the Draganora Hotel for lunch (or light dinner if it was an evening game). They would have to choose from a set menu of energy-giving, carbohydrate-based meals, usually pasta. (The management – of course – were exempt. We all had fish suppers!)

All the players were doing their best to follow the dietitian's advice. All except one that is. One morning, I bumped into Mickey coming into the ground. Shooting the breeze, I asked him what he'd had for his dinner last night. "Tripe and chips, chairman, same as always," came the reply. It seemed against the home-cooked meals lovingly served up by Mickey's mum, our dietitian stood no chance.

Around this time, Mickey was getting some grief off the pitch. Edinburgh is not the easiest of cities in which to be famous, and fans of rival teams would abuse him when he was out in the town. I remember hearing that his new car had been smashed by vandals who hurled a can of paint over it for good measure. No sooner had Mickey replaced the car, it happened again. Mickey told us that he needed to get away. Alex had come to see Mickey as a bit of a luxury player. Mickey wanted to be on the attack all the time. Patterns of play and team shape were not his forte at all. When Luton Town made an approach, Alex was more than happy to let the boy go.

Having sailed through his medical and agreed terms with Hatters manager Ray Harford, Mickey moved south (in 1987). His new club encouraged him to buy a house in Bedfordshire. He asked me to do his conveyancing and, in so doing, became my client. He had worked for me, and now I would serve him.

In no time, Mickey started to miss his friends and family and was homesick for Edinburgh, the only place he'd ever lived. He also later told me that he particularly longed for the green, green grass at Easter Road as Luton played on an appalling plastic pitch. Having made a bright start at Luton – who were on their way to winning the English League Cup that season – Mickey Weir wanted to come home.

Mickey reminded me of one of my favourite players, John Robertson, who was world class for Nottingham Forest and Scotland. Martin Edwards once told me a lovely story he'd heard from someone at the City Ground. During a practice match, Robertson had kept coming infield trying to retrieve the ball. When this happened for the umpteenth time, Brian Clough – observing from the side of the pitch – called out in that cutting nasal voice of his, "Young man, stop it. All this football club and the people of Nottingham need from you is to run down the bloody wing, turn the full-back inside out and put crosses in. There are players here paid to do the dirty work. You are not one of them."

I felt Mickey could do a similar job for us as we tried to get to the top of Scottish football. Others at the club took the view that you never take a player back. Jim had his doubts, Alex even more so. But they came around to my way of thinking.

Less than three months on from our last meeting with Ray Harford, we reconvened. We agreed to pay the exact same fee that we had received for Mickey to bring him home. There must have been at least one estate agent in Luton that did very nicely out of Mickey's brief stay at Kenilworth Road.

Wee Mickey would play for Hibs until 1996, making a further 158 appearances and scoring 25 goals. He did venture south one more time, loaned to Millwall, but only managed eight games. The Mickey Weir story is about loving your home, family and community. Hibernian Football Club was a massive part of that for Mickey.

*

There would come a time when Wallace Mercer would accuse Hibs fans of tribalism in opposing his bid. Football is tribal but not in the negative way Wallace saw it.

Doctors, lawyers and powerful men sit alongside workmen and the unemployed, policemen and criminals, sinners and saints, saints and sinners, all together, one tribe, for 90 magical minutes. What else but football brings these people together in our society? Wearing the same coloured jerseys and scarves, singing in unity, supporting their team. We need to belong. It is without doubt pure tribalism. But what is wrong with that?

David Rowland did not understand this. Nor did Wallace Mercer. How could he if he thought that by calling Hibs fans tribal, he was insulting them? Coming from him, the chairman of Hearts, it was a huge compliment.

THREE

WALLACE

EDINBURGH IS A wee town in many ways. The population today is touching half a million. That is smaller than Sheffield. It is, however, a financial powerhouse, home to the Royal Bank and the Bank of Scotland, and where the likes of Standard Life and Scottish Widows flourish. Beyond these grand institutions, there are a small number of powerful men who control wealth and commerce. Some are household names, while others live quietly in the shadows. They do not welcome strange fish into their pool. Wallace Mercer was one of the best connected.

The Masonic movement is strong in Scotland. My own father was a Grand Master of the Easter Road lodge. I hope I didn't disappoint him by not following him into the craft. On the other side of the religious divide, the Catholic community had their own tight business network with a strict hierarchy. In both, those with power seek to maintain the status quo. Football was the arena where these communities openly clashed.

During my first year at Hibs, I did not get to know Wallace Mercer very well. We did not frequent the same places. Except, on the odd Friday, when Wallace enjoyed a boys' night out with his pals from the property world at the very fashionable Cosmo restaurant where Sean Connery was a regular patron. Whenever I was in town ahead of the weekend, I would join the Hibs' super-executive club at a table there that just happened to be close to Wallace's. Of the two parties, we were much the rowdier. We would often send drinks over to them. They would reply in kind, although I'm pretty sure Wallace didn't approve.

The Hearts chairman hosted his own radio and television shows for a while around this time and confessed to being a "controlled egomaniac". My experience of him was that away from the media spotlight, he was shy and a little awkward. I was once invited over to his table at Cosmo by a well-known Edinburgh surveyor for a chat. While Wallace's mates urged me to sit down and have a drink, he turned away. He was not rude but uncomfortable. Perhaps we brought out the worst in each other. I've met plenty of people over the years who have told me they always found Wallace great company. But at the time, I formed the view that the man's egotism was driven by deep insecurity. After all, he drove a Jaguar with the number plate XX1. It had to be explained to me that the message it carried was DOUBLE-CROSS ONE. Why anyone would want to portray themselves as a double-crosser, I do not know.

He had nothing to fear from me. I was a Scotsman based in England and had no interest in joining the Edinburgh business clique. I believe his fear was that I would make Hibs the biggest club in the capital. I held the view that this was already the case, so in that sense, I never really considered us to be in competition.

Sometimes on a derby day, we would both be interviewed by Radio Forth. I really enjoyed the challenge and chance to show off my knowledge of the game. On one occasion, Wallace came into the studio wearing a white Hearts pullover with maroon braiding. Under the breast pocket, stitched in the same colour, lived the legendary words: "Wallace Mercer".

I always came to the radio casually dressed. I'm a natural scruff. "Are you wearing that in case you forget your name?" I quipped. I was just being friendly. Wallace, furious, blanked me. He refused all subsequent offers to be interviewed together on Radio Forth. He did not want to share a platform with me. I couldn't imagine then that a day was approaching when I would be invited on stage by Wallace to legitimise his plan to bury Hibernian.

One derby day at Tynecastle, the sponsors of the game were British Telecom. Wallace and I were to be presented with 'state-of-the-art' handsets. They even came with answerphones. Wallace refused to allow the ceremony at half-time, forcing the sponsors to present our telephones in front of an empty stand after the match. Only two of Wallace's favoured journalists witnessed the sorry spectacle. (Ironically, my phone never worked.)

On another occasion, Wallace and I were asked to plant a tree sapling at the Holiday Inn on Queensferry Road. The *Evening News* took photos. It must have been a very slow news day! A few years ago, I went back to see if the tree I'd planted had survived. I was surprised by how moved I was to find that not only was it still standing but that it had thrived.

There is a perception among some fans that Wallace and I were arch enemies. That is not true. I hardly knew the man. What I can say is that visits to Tynecastle were never pleasant. The away dressing room was tiny and housed next to an ancient boiler. It was oven-hot in there no matter the time of year. The boardroom was sterile and without fun. Nearly every time we played there, one of our staff or players would be reported to the police for something spurious. Often it was petty. Every conceivable opportunity to make our visit unpleasant seemed to be taken with relish by Hearts. It would start as soon as we arrived. We were ordered to park the team coach about 70 yards from the stadium entrance, forcing us to walk through an area open to the Hearts fans. The abuse was so bad we decided to start bringing our own security escort.

Had Wallace got his way and formed Edinburgh United, it would have represented Scottish football's biggest contradiction. Edinburgh was anything but united.

*

For all my faults, I like to think I was a very different chairman to Wallace Mercer. Chairmen tended to be older gentlemen in this era, keen to erect strict barriers between the boardroom and dressing room. Few were lifelong supporters of the football clubs they owned – I often wondered whether Wallace loved the game in the same way I did. I'm sure he'd have been the first to admit he relished the profile the Hearts chairmanship gave him. Most of the others had never stood on the terraces as schoolboys. That's what I had done, and as a result, I felt the club's victories and defeats all the more keenly.

One of the awful statistics I inherited was that we had not beaten our Edinburgh rivals, Hearts, since 1979. Playing four times a season, this equated to many hours of misery for our fans. I decided after the game at Tynecastle – which saw Alan Rough's last appearance in the Edinburgh derby – that this couldn't go on. I looked at the fixture list and resolved the unwanted streak would end on Saturday, 17 October, 1987, my first home game against the old enemy. I invited my friends and family to Easter Road, such was my confidence, promising that we would celebrate a great win after the game.

I decided to incentivise the boys with a "chairman's bonus", and the players were on an extra £1,000 each for the win. Nothing but victory would do. Just before the game, in a showy demonstration of my unwavering belief in the team, I arranged for four bottles of the best champagne to be deposited in the manager's fridge. This was to be done conspicuously in full view of the players. There would be little need for a team talk.

It was a beautiful, sunny autumn afternoon, and there were 23,890 supporters packed into Easter Road, a capacity crowd. It took Eddie May just three minutes to give us the lead, and although John Robertson equalised, Paul Kane had us ahead again by half-time. The second half was a nervous affair, but, by now, we had Andy Goram. There was no way that day anything else was getting past him. We won 2-1 and a decade of hurt was over.

After Saturday games, Jim and I would take our wives for a meal, usually Italian food. On this night, we were clapped to our table. The wine was on the house. A player, who shall remain nameless, revealed to me later that he had won a good wad of money by betting on us to win. He explained that as "you lot upstairs" had such faith in the team, he should believe too.

These were small but significant steps in leaving behind the perception that we were the downtrodden poor relations of Edinburgh football. The club had a supporters' association under which sat various supporters' clubs. Each held dinners and events throughout the season. Early on, I made it known that Jim and I would consider it an honour to attend such events. I was particularly touched to receive an invite from the Carlton Branch, where I had been a teenage member. They presented me with a gift that I cherish to this day.

The most memorable visit, however, was to the Craigmillar Supporters' Club. Craigmillar is on the south-east side of town and is a sprawling council estate. It has a reputation for being one of the toughest areas of Edinburgh. It was also the Hibs heartland. I don't think any past director had visited these supporters' clubs, but I know for certain I was the first to venture into Craigmillar on a Saturday evening. I arrived at the event in my green Mercedes, registration number HIB51, which I parked outside the community centre. No one keyed the chairman's car that day. I was treated like royalty. Embarrassingly, I even won the raffle and was politely but firmly rebuffed when I tried to put the prize back. As far as I know, it hadn't been a fix.

Just after 11pm, the chair of the Craigmillar branch took me aside. "Mr Chairman," he said. "We will always be grateful to you for coming, but we think you should go home now. Everyone has been on their best behaviour so far, but things might get a bit wild now. We are not used to being this restrained, and we wouldn't want you to think badly of us." I slipped away, smiling to myself. Not even the chairman of Hibernian could tame the Craigmillar supporters.

The pace was a little slower in our new super executive club. There we had a member called Gordon Scott. Scottish Gordon had married into one of Edinburgh's Italian restaurant families. He ran a restaurant incongruously called Gordon's Trattoria on the High Street. It is still there today. Gordon became friendly with many of the squad and his restaurant assumed legendary status with players and fans alike.

It was the place to be on a Wednesday night after a game. I used to go there myself, and I'd always find a player or two there tucking into a plate of pasta and happy to share football stories. Gordon's was a place we could all let our hair down, somewhere we could be ourselves. Our fans absolutely loved having contact with the players, and credit to the boys, they reciprocated this warmth. We never had any grumbles from the first-teamers when we asked them to attend Hibernian Supporters' Club functions. We were trying to renew the links between the club and its community. It is what Hibs had been founded on but had somehow lost. Businessmen, players, die-hard fans, old men and children were falling in behind their club. It was heartening to see attendances at Easter Road starting to improve.

There were old traditions that had to be respected too. Every Friday, the fishmonger would deliver me a packet of fish. The headmaster of the Catholic school and the local priest were also recipients of this gift. I loved the custom. This had nothing to do with sectarianism, but instead reflected the pride people felt in their own community.

I perhaps hadn't fully grasped this distinction when, early on, we changed the club badge. Out went the crown and Irish harp to be replaced with a 'Juventus-style' modern logo. Tradition is part of the lifeblood of a football club, and I know the change upset some fans. In our defence, I should explain that the initial stimulus for the new design came from outside the club. The Court of the Lord Lyon notified us that we were not entitled to have the Scottish crown on our crest. Sadly, though, I have to hold my hands up for approving the terrible 'beer bottle badge'. I think the 'new' Hibs crest is perfect, beautifully combining both the club's Edinburgh and Irish origins. For me, Hibernian are a Leith team, open to everyone, but also passionately proud of our past.

FOUR

TRANSFER COUPS AND COCK-UPS

OUR FANS, AND the tabloids, were in complete agreement that having already signed Neil Orr, a midfielder, Hibs urgently needed a new striker. It came as a surprise to us all, therefore, when Alex Miller asked to further reinforce the middle of the park. Even more of a shock was that the man in question played for Hearts.

Andy Watson had a wise head on young shoulders. He was a dedicated trainer and was totally committed in every game. Sadly he was at a disadvantage, having come from our cross-town rivals, and some of the supporters did not take to him. One morning about a year after Andy signed, I arrived at Easter Road for a meeting to find him sitting outside the main stand. I was very concerned as he was sobbing. He had just been told his career was prematurely over because of injury. I had no idea that the condition that had been keeping him out of the team was that serious. We sat in the sun, reflecting on just how cruel life could be, and I tried to encourage him to stay in the game. With his knowledge of football and vision for how the game should be played, I thought he would make a fine coach. I suggested he take his SFA coaching badges.

Andy feared that now he could no longer play, he would be pitched out of the club into unemployment. In our discussion, I overstepped the mark somewhat, all but offering him a place on the coaching staff. This was not in my remit, but I said I would put the idea to Alex. And if he agreed, the directors would be in full support. I immediately raised the matter at our next board meeting. My argument was that Andy could be an asset as he would find common ground with young players easily. Also, aged just 29, he would be gaining a head start on his contemporaries in qualifying as a coach. It would be a win-win. Usually, managers are fiercely protective when it comes to their backroom teams, but Alex liked Andy and was enthusiastic about keeping him on. It turned out well. Andy and Alex would work together in years to come at the very highest level of the game.

Many years later, I was sitting behind the dugout at Hampden for a Scotland game. There, next to the national team manager Alex McLeish, was Andy Watson. I watched Andy for some time and must admit I felt no small pride, seeing how he'd bounced back from that day I'd found him shattered outside Easter Road. Of course, Andy achieved all he did on his own merit. But I was pleased that in some way, we at Hibs gave him his start.

*

One of the privileges of being a younger chairman was that, from time to time, the opportunity arose to play a game of football with my childhood heroes. Gotham City, the Hibs staff team, did not play many matches, but in its ranks was a mixture of old pros and youngsters that the management wanted toughening up.

Jim and I were given the honour of playing one day, and I got the nod to start up top. Whether me being the chairman influenced the team selection, I cannot possibly say. During the first half, the opposition goal was never in any danger. I ran about cluelessly, playing alongside a youngster of real promise. I am sure he recounted with relish to the rest of the youth team afterwards that the chairman of Hibs is the worst strike partner he'd ever played with.

Andy Watson, no longer able to play professionally, was still fit enough to anchor the Gotham midfield. I remember being singularly unimpressed by his performance that day. He plonked ball after ball over my head, far in front of me. I decided that he must have lost some of his sharpness and that his passing radar was waning. After the game, we adjourned to the bar of a small hotel – it was a Sunday, so Scottish pubs were closed for the Sabbath. My legs were burning, and I was in a grump. "Hey, Andy!" I said, "those passes you were giving me were terrible. I think you have lost your touch." "Sorry, chairman," he replied. "But to be fair, I'm used to forwards who run into space rather than the opposition defenders." I've never forgotten that brilliant retort. Andy was alright for a 'jam tart'.

Regrettably, not all the memories I have of time spent with the players are happy ones. On one Saturday morning, before a Tynecastle derby, I sat with the first team watching our reserves take on Hearts' second string in a warm-up for the main event. Suddenly, an over-the-top tackle on Danny Lennon resulted in a resounding crack echoing sickeningly around the empty ground.

The referee, who must have been the only person in the stadium not to hear it, mysteriously played on, leaving Hearts to score. By then, however, our players and staff who were watching from the sidelines had run on to the pitch. Andy was leading the charge. When Danny Lennon, who was at the beginning of his career, was carried off, I was horrified to see the state of his leg. His foot was facing the wrong direction. It took about a year, but Danny did come back, although he never quite realised the great promise he had shown at Hibs before the injury. I am pleased to say he has since gone on to have a successful career as a manager, most recently at Clyde. A couple of seasons ago, he even made a brief onfield return – debuting for the injury-ravaged Bully Wee against Celtic Colts at the tender age of 50.

It is a testament to Alex Miller that many of his former players made their mark as coaches. Nearly all of them were midfielders.

*

I came to believe that our manager thought that the best form of attack was defence. Alex's teams were built from the back, and there was a perception that he played negative football. In defence of Alex, he had done a fine job at St Mirren before coming to Hibs, steering them well clear of relegation trouble while finishing above us in the table. And, when he first came to the club before our arrival, the resources at his disposal undoubtedly put a limit on his ambition. But I now wanted him to get the club punching upwards instead of looking down. My job was to convince Alex that Hibs could achieve more. We needed to achieve more. The need for a striker or two in the squad was becoming desperate. I began to hear cries of "Get your cheque book out, Duff!" from fans at home matches, so long had they waited for a bona-fide goal-scorer to arrive at Easter Road.

Alex preferred forwards who defended from the front or midfielders who could score goals. His assistant Peter Cormack, on the other hand, wanted a penalty-box predator. I enjoyed talking to Peter. It was a treat for me as when I was a boy, he had been my hero. I would ask him about his time playing for Bill Shankly and sat entranced as he told me the story of his transfer from Nottingham Forest to Anfield.

It was 1972 and, just before the season started, Peter was handed a train ticket from Nottingham to Liverpool. It was

Forest's way of telling him he was being sold. In those days, players had no power over their destinies. Until the train arrived at Lime Street, Peter wasn't even sure if he was joining Everton or Liverpool! There on the platform, waiting for him as he stepped down from the carriage, were two gentlemen in red blazers.

Peter recounted his first encounter with Bill Shankly to me. The great Ayrshire motivator explained how he'd been tracking Peter for years based on a glowing recommendation from his brother. Bob Shankly had been Peter's manager at Easter Road for four years in the 1960s.

"You, son, are the player I need to make Liverpool Football Club perfection." Barely able to contain his pride, Peter waited for the great man's next piece of wisdom. "What have you been doing for pre-season training over there in Nottingham?" asked Shanks. "We've been running through the woods and doing weights, Mr Shankly." "Running through the trees?" Shankly repeated to himself incredulously, before quipping, "Here at Liverpool, we leave that to the squirrels."

Beyond being a great storyteller, I could see that just like his old boss at Anfield, Peter had a keen eye for talent. He was always comfortable making suggestions to the board about potential new players, and I was happy to listen. Alex, by contrast, did not think chairmen should have any input into transfers. To a certain extent, I suppose, he was right. I would have been pretty nonplussed if he'd lectured me on how to run the business side of the club. Alex would repeatedly say, "The signing of players is a matter for the manager and the managing director alone. No one else." Peter and I would have to hold our wee chats discreetly.

Despite these occasional tensions between the dugout and boardroom, we all wanted the same thing: a great Hibernian. With the quest for a centre forward ongoing, we decided to dust off our secret weapon. Martin put in the call to brother

Ferguson, enquiring if Manchester United knew of any players worth a look for not more than £300,000.

We were tipped off that a recent Youth Training Scheme graduate at Preston North End was available for a very reasonable fee. The player, we were told, had real potential. Over Christmas, Jim and I decided to take Peter Cormack to see him play. Maybe we could convince Alex to take a gamble. On 28 December, 1987, the youngster was scheduled to be playing away at Sunderland. We drove down from Edinburgh for the holiday match.

I have always enjoyed festive football. It serves as a fullblooded antidote to the suspended animation that life becomes at that time of year. This was just as well because when we were handed the team sheets, Nigel Jemson, the player we were there to see, hadn't made the starting XI. In one sense, it was a wasted trip. But such journeys are never really made in vain for football fans. Peter plied us with more of his great stories throughout the match. We watched a 1-1 draw and retired to a boardroom full of legendary names. None more so than Bob Stokoe, who had managed Sunderland when the Second Division club rocked the mighty Leeds United in the 1973 FA Cup final. Stokoe was no longer the Sunderland manager but was there as an honoured club guest. Later in my tenure, I would meet Ian Porterfield, the player who scored the Wembley winning goal, a name few fans of my generation will forget. We had lost the opportunity to make the case to Alex about Nigel Jemson, and Nottingham Forest swooped in. Jemson subsequently scored a Wembley winner in the 1990 League Cup final and was capped for England under-21s. He also achieved the dubious honour of being described by Brian Clough as "the only player with a head bigger than mine".

So determined was I to sign a striker, we even pursued the possibility of bringing Justin Fashanu back to British football from America. We did lots of research contacting his previous clubs, who were all oddly reluctant to talk about him. Finally, we called

Brian Clough, asking him whether he could shine a light on Justin and why he had gone so spectacularly off the boil. Cloughie, not one for anything approaching political correctness, offered little opinion on his football and instead went on a rant about the player attending gay bars and nightclubs in Nottingham. I won't repeat his actual words. None of that put me off. But again, Alex wasn't interested. Justin did eventually have a brief and unhappy spell playing in Edinburgh, scoring one goal for Hearts during a handful of games at Tynecastle in the early 90s.

As the search went on, Alex Ferguson came up with some other striking names, but at the top of his list of recommendations was an attacking midfielder. "He'll score you goals for fun." Having been released by Manchester United as a youngster, the player was now making headlines at Crewe Alexandra. Fergie was sure the boy could excel for us and knew that Crewe were willing to sell. Other clubs were interested, and we needed to move quickly. Alex Miller insisted on watching the player himself before initiating any deal. Crewe had a game on the coming Wednesday evening, but so did we. Alex wanted to be with his team, so Peter was dispatched south of the border on a scouting mission.

We were in the boardroom after our game when Peter called with his verdict. He raved about the player impressing on us that we needed to make a decision immediately, or we'd miss out. Alex was reluctant to buy someone he had never seen in the flesh, but we eventually agreed to submit a bid. An offer of £150,000 was sent to Crewe by fax. We reached a verbal agreement. Provisional arrangements were made for the player to travel to Edinburgh for a medical and to discuss personal terms the next day.

Peter had travelled home after the Crewe match. Despite his late night, he joined the rest of us at Easter Road the next morning in anticipation of us completing the signing. If anything, his enthusiasm for the lad had only grown stronger. The fax machine suddenly jolted into life. It was a message from

Crewe. Overnight, Aston Villa had made an offer for the player of £250,000. And, as Crewe were not a rich club, they couldn't turn it down. Embarrassed, the Crewe chairman said that, as a compromise, if we would up our bid to £200,000, the boy would be ours. An argument then broke out between Peter and Alex. Peter urged us to pay the extra money while Alex refused to go a penny above the £150,000 offered the night before. Their views were so polarised that to overrule Alex would have meant sacking him. We decided we had to back his judgement.

David Platt signed for Aston Villa later that day. He was 22 years old at the time. Platt went on to play 121 times for Villa, helping them to promotion in his first season. Under Bobby Robson, he became an England favourite, excelling at World Cup 1990 and later captaining his country. In a glittering career, he played for Bari, Juventus and Sampdoria, before returning to England as part of Arsène Wenger's magnificent 1998 double-winning Arsenal team. For me, David Platt will always be the one that got away. He really was a mere fax from becoming a Hibs player. Alex Ferguson had been spot on. Platt could score with both feet and his head. And although he was a midfielder, he surely would have solved our problems. Hibs had still not found their goal-scorer.

*

I did manage to get one cracking deal over the line that winter, although I quickly came to regret it. The draw for round three of the Scottish Cup paired Hibs with Dumbarton, taking me to the wonderfully named Boghead Park for the first time on 30 January, 1988. This was a new boardroom for me, and I was keen to hear all their directors' gossip. Dumbarton had been owned by Sir Hugh Fraser, the department store proprietor, who had recently passed away. His daughter, Patricia, was heir apparent, but she had no interest in football. As I chatted with her, I cheekily asked what she would want for her shares. I was surprised it was somewhere south of £100,000.

An idea was beginning to form. Why don't I buy the club for my father? My dad absolutely loved football – he had been a great Hibs man dating back to his childhood before the war, and my love of the club was passed to me through my love for him. At this stage of his life, I thought he'd get a massive kick out of running a club of his own. Looking back, it was an ostentatious gesture on my part bordering on arrogance.

After a draw and a winning replay at Easter Road, I opened negotiations and bought the club, putting the shares in his name. The whole thing was done at warp speed. Dumbarton's existing board contained a director of the Tennent's Brewery, who Dad installed as chairman. He was enjoying it and spent a lot of time there. Had things worked out differently, it might have been his business for the rest of his life.

Scottish football is a small world, and Graeme Souness came to play an unlikely role in how events unfolded at Boghead. The Rangers manager lived in Edinburgh in a 'Hacienda-style' home he'd built in Colinton, in the shadow of the Pentland Hills. It was a strange house, with two wings jutting from a glass-fronted centre, tiled floors and a horse paddock. While it might have looked great in Spain, it was most certainly out of place in this well-to-do Edinburgh suburb. I believe Graeme's then-wife, Danielle, was brought up on Majorca, and this had obviously influenced her style. Theirs was a stormy marriage, which split around the time we played at Boghead. By coincidence, Graeme started to date Patricia Fraser and asked her what she planned to do with Dumbarton. When she told him that she had sold the shares to me, Graeme immediately informed Jim Farry, the all-powerful secretary of the Scottish League. At this time the long-established structure of British football was coming under strain in various quarters. For example, in England Robert Maxwell was testing the rules of club ownership and governance to their limit.

Jim Farry was a regular in our boardroom for meetings with our Jim, Jim Gray, who had been elected to the League Committee. Farry knew how to find me, so I expected his call if he had a problem with the Dumbarton deal. I really had bought the club for my father, so I was ready to have a row if it came to it. My phone never rang, but events inevitably came to a head.

Back then, when a player was called up for Scotland, it was customary for representatives of his club to receive an invite to watch the match with officials from the SFA and Scottish League. If you had two players in the squad, the club received two invites and so on.

On one such Wednesday evening, Jim and I were invited to The Albany Hotel in Glasgow for the pre-match meal. I'm sorry to confess, we were a little late in arriving. We went into the basement reception where, sitting alone, we found Kenny Dalglish – one of the finest players I have ever seen play the game. For all his achievements, he remains a modest gentleman, with time for everyone. After a quick chat, I said to Kenny, "We're going into the function room. Are you coming?" Kenny explained that he had been barred from entry and told to sit in reception. Liverpool only had one player in the squad and, therefore, only one ticket for the dinner. Typically, Kenny had given his ticket to an old school friend who was not involved with football beyond being a fanatical member of the Tartan Army. As a "courtesy", Scotland's greatest ever player had been told he would, at least, be allowed to travel on the bus taking the delegation to Hampden. I was surprised that Kenny had been, apparently, bounced from the dinner. But that surprise turned into confusion when inside I found the meal was not a sit-down affair with limited places but a buffet.

Committee members from all levels of Scottish football mixed eating lobster and Mediterranean prawns, while 'King

Kenny' sat outside. I found Jim Farry and advised him as to what was going on. He already knew. "Who does he think he is, giving a hospitality ticket to someone outside the game?" "Kenny Dalglish," I replied. This encapsulated everything I felt was wrong with Scottish football at the time. I can only hope things at the top of the game have now changed. When we boarded the bus to Hampden, Jim was engrossed in deep conversation with a fellow committee member, so I sat on my own at the front. Looking out the window as the police motorbikes whisked us through the heavy Glasgow traffic, I suddenly became aware that Farry was headed my way. As he lowered himself into the seat next to me, I assumed he was about to make peace following the Dalglish affair. Instead, we sat in total silence for the duration of the journey. Then, finally, as the coach pulled up at the national stadium, he turned to me and said, "Mr Duff: Sell Dumbarton."

Within a short time, as I shall explain later, I needed my parents to step in and support me by running a chain of pubs in the West of England that Hibs had come to own. My dad sold his stake at Boghead to a Falkirk teacher who said it was his dream to become a football club owner. I knew the feeling.

A few weeks after the Dumbarton game on 17 February, 1988, I celebrated my 34th birthday. On the same day, John Collins won his first Scotland cap. He travelled to Saudi Arabia and crowned his debut with a beautiful curling free-kick in a 2-2 draw. When John returned, he gave me a present I have always treasured. As I look up from my desk, there framed is a beautiful blue number 11 Scotland jersey. Next to it is a shirt that Andy Goram wore on international duty that he had all his teammates sign for me. The stories I would often read in the English press maligning footballers for their behaviour both on and off the pitch never rang true for me. The players at Hibs were capable of the most incredible grace and kindness.

FIVE

BOARDROOMS, BOMBS AND ARCHIE

NON-LEAGUE KETTERING Town were the unlikely pioneers of shirt sponsorship in football. In January 1976, their players took to the field for a game with Bath City with the name of a local tyre firm emblazoned across their chests. During the 1980s, shirt sponsorship was becoming an increasingly lucrative source of clubs' income. The bigger the team, the bigger the deal. Before then, live football on television had been restricted to cup finals and international matches. Soon, television would take over the game. Within a few years of my arrival at Hibs, matches were being beamed across the planet.

For a time, in some competitions, television companies would not allow sponsors' names to appear on jerseys. The BBC did not allow televised advertising, and ITV sought to protect their own commercial clients. Clubs had to produce an alternative 'blank' strip for use in TV matches. In October 1980, a game between Aston Villa and Brighton was cancelled because both sides refused to play, having been banned from wearing sponsored strips. Eventually, the broadcasters relented. And by the 1987/88 season, every team in the English Football League and most in Scotland had a sponsor.

When I took over at Hibs, there was an existing agreement with a double-glazing firm called P&D Windows. Double-glazing sponsorship was all the rage in Scottish football. The Old Firm's shirts bore the name CR Smith. I always thought it was telling that despite their antipathy towards each other, the two sides of Glasgow managed to find commercial common ground. Of course, this made absolute business sense as no company wanted to alienate half of the city's population. It would have been great to reach such an arrangement with Hearts, but frankly, there was no meaningful dialogue between the clubs.

We decided not to renew the P&D Windows contract. This meant we played out the remainder of the 1987/88 season with sponsor-less shirts until a suitable new partner could be found. The board wanted a local brand of integrity that had a genuine affinity with Hibernian. Raymond Sparkes, Jim Gray and I were of one mind as we weighed up our options. The Frank Graham Group, rather than being an eclectic mix of jazz musicians, was a firm building fine Edinburgh homes. They were growing fast and were prepared to enter into a three-year deal worth four times more than the previous sponsors'. For the time, this represented a good slice of the club's overall income.

The company was owned and run by two brothers, Frank and Robert. They were self-made men, and I suppose the attraction to Hibs was founded in their love of football. In truth, Frank was a dyed-in-the-wool Celtic supporter. But – apart from when we played The Hoops when he kept diplomatically quiet in a private box that we laid on especially – he was a passionate ambassador for our club. After games, either he or his brother, Robert, would come up to the super executive club and present the 'Man of the Match' award. The Frank Graham Group would later fade away, victims of the recession that bit hard in the early 1990s. But for this time we were proud to promote them. I am sure Frank would have been tickled to know that our jerseys bearing his name now fetch a fortune on eBay. During the early months of the Covid-19 pandemic, I noticed someone was even knocking out Hibs Frank Graham Group kit design face masks for sale.

Support for the club was not limited to the Edinburgh business community. The convenor of Lothian District Council, Jimmy Cook, was determined to throw his support behind Hibs. He became a regular guest in our boardroom. Politically savvy, on the Saturdays when we weren't at home Jimmy could be found enjoying Wallace Mercer's hospitality at Tynecastle. The story goes he would canvas voters around Easter Road in a Hearts scarf. Such was the respect for the man, he never encountered any hostility in Leith. Jimmy was a visionary who dreamed of seeing trams return to Edinburgh. Although sadly not in his lifetime, at the cost of many millions of pounds and much political wrangling, his wish came true. Jimmy's obituary would confirm once and for all that Hearts was his real footballing passion. But he loved his city above all else and prized both its great football clubs.

Before the end of the season, we made a three-way announcement where the Frank Graham Group, Lothian Region and the club unveiled a new partnership. The resulting publicity was very favourable towards Hibs. And on the back of it, we tried to exploit any and every commercial opportunity we could think of.

As we entered the final weeks of the 1987/88 campaign, I realised how much I had learnt about the workings of professional football. I came to understand that the most diverse and challenging job in the game is that of club secretary. Among myriad other duties, the secretary is responsible for ensuring that all the players' registrations are valid and knowing every intricacy of any transfer deal. Many a club has come a cropper for fielding an ineligible player – Hibs did this as recently as July 2022 in a League Cup tie with Morton. When a team is expelled from a competition for this kind of error, the club secretary is always blamed. There are precious few occasions when he is lauded, but his diligence and discretion are integral to any successful football club. Our secretary was Cecil Graham, and he was one of the best. He was a massive Hibs fan and never let us down. Cecil passed on in 2018. If his family ever read this, please accept my thanks for his immeasurable contribution to Hibernian Football Club.

Cecil had contacts everywhere in the game. If I ever wanted to go to a match, he would work his magic and somehow wangle me boardroom entrance or corporate hospitality seats. If we were not playing midweek, I would take in an English fixture, sometimes two. This helped me to read a game, showed me what other clubs were doing and sparked ideas. After a while, I became part of a set that would always attend the same matches. The group included Ron Atkinson and Don Howe – an unmatchable coach – plus several English football chairmen. We were a strange bunch. I learnt so much about football from just sitting and listening to their stories.

I was also invited to do a regular news review for Great Western Radio, my local commercial radio station in Swindon. Each week, I would pick out two or three unusual stories from the newspapers and give my take. I had to go to the studio in Wootton Bassett early in the morning for the recordings. In future seasons, one of the other regular contributors was the Swindon Town manager, Ossie Ardiles. The County Ground became a favourite place to visit because of Ossie's warmth and hospitality. Sometimes, GWR would ask me to accompany their reporter to matches and offer an opinion on the action.

On one such occasion when Swindon played Watford at Vicarage Road, the club secretary asked me if I'd like to meet the directors at half-time rather than return to the press box. I couldn't accept fast enough hoping one man, in particular, might be there. Entering what appeared a typical boardroom, I spied a door in the middle of the back wall. A steward escorted me into a secret room that lay on the other side. Inside sat only two people – an elderly woman and, wearing a baseball cap and sunglasses, her son. I was suddenly face-to-face with Elton John. Once I'd managed to articulate some actual words, we chatted about football and shared experiences of running a club. I was gutted when it was time for the second half to start. I was only in the great man's presence for a few minutes, but it's an experience I will never forget. If only there had been smartphones and selfies back then.

*

Travelling around the great stadiums of British football, I was shocked at how replica shirts and memorabilia were sold. Clubs put in so little effort. Even the great Manchester United were selling their wares from a portacabin. Mail order was in its infancy, and online shopping a long way off. Witnessing the demand from fans and recognising that merchandising could be a vast source of income, I thought: why not have a Hibs store? We leased a shop near Easter Road. Basically, if you could put a Hibernian badge on it, we sold it. Today you will see Rangers and Celtic shops in most Scottish town centres, but I believe Hibs had the first high-street club store in Scotland.

It struck me that English clubs, in particular, banned from European competition since 1985, were being left behind by their continental rivals. Hibs had endured a self-imposed exile from the European game. We had not qualified for Europe in a decade, and I vowed this had to change. I remembered great Hibernian European nights from my youth, including one at Elland Road that I had attended when I was a student. For me, then and now, Hibs belong on the European stage.

Of course, I wanted to win the league, the Scottish Cup, the League Cup and every other game we played but, as an absolute minimum, we had to restore European football to Easter Road. The roadmap to take us there required we keep pushing ahead with our commercial plan.

During our first season, the Easter Road boardroom on a match day became one of the liveliest venues in Edinburgh, even if I do say so myself. Reflecting on our negative experiences at Tynecastle Park, I wanted everyone enjoying Hibs' hospitality to have a belting time. Even if they were supporting our opponents.

I even managed to get David Rowland to come along to a few games. I think Easter Road may have been the first football stadium he'd ever visited. He could see how much his former wife Sheila and his children enjoyed the Hibs experience. Surely, some of this would rub off? He'd see Hibs were for keeps, and honour his as yet unfulfilled promise to deliver the Scottish properties that would underpin our income.

Former England captain Johnny Haynes was often a guest in the boardroom. When I was a boy, I'd watched him playing for Fulham. I remember him becoming Britain's first £100 a week player and how a terrible car accident on the Blackpool promenade had robbed him of the England captaincy. Edinburgh was Johnny's adopted home, and while I was more than a little star-struck when I first met him, he proved fabulous company. Other regulars were future Labour chancellor Alistair Darling, and even Hector Clark, the deputy chief constable of Lothian Police. A handy person to know, as I'll explain shortly. Wives and girlfriends were always welcome too. They were often more passionate and knowledgeable about the team than their other halves.

It was Jim and Cecil's job to make sure we could accommodate all our guests, and I must have driven them crazy. I have a big family and constantly made last-minute requests for seats. Jim would protest but somehow found a way to squeeze everyone in. Cecil ended up holding back a couple of places to ensure I didn't inadvertently give away the spots required for the opposition chairman and manager. The capacity was dictated by the number of seats in the boardroom's viewing box. I would have stood on the roof to watch Hibs. On a few occasions, that almost became necessary, especially when the big teams were in town.

The fact that we were still entertaining an hour after the game, leaving visiting players waiting on the bus for their directors, became a badge of honour for me. Hearts were the only opposing team who didn't seem to enjoy our hospitality. They couldn't make their getaway fast enough. In fairness to them, we felt the same whenever we visited their place.

Other clubs had their own style of hospitality. I only visited Morton once but was welcomed by three older gentlemen who insisted on arrival that I enjoy a rare single malt whisky. I don't like the national drink, but out of courtesy took a small dram and then another. My glass never emptied, and I saw the game through double vision. Hospitality in Aberdeen was based on the old adage: "you'll have had your tea". A corner cabinet was reluctantly opened, from which you were offered a solitary glass of beer or carefully measured whisky along with a Scotch pie cut into quarters. The cabinet was then immediately locked shut.

Dundee chairman Angus Cook was always a good visit. Angus was a natural host and a bit of a showman. If you looked closely at the pinstripe in his suit, it revealed and repeated his name in tiny red thread. Even Wallace Mercer didn't go that far. Dundee United, by contrast, was a tense experience. The directors' box was behind glass and deathly quiet. We would be forced to listen to the legendary but irascible Jim McLean's comments throughout the game. After two visits, fearing for my life, I insisted on taking a ticket in the stands. I enjoyed visiting Dunfermline, where Mel Rennie and the vivacious Jim Leishman were tremendous hosts. They also did the best pies in Scotland. Motherwell and Hamilton were traditional and pleasant.

And then there were the big two. I always felt welcome at

Celtic. Every game I went to at Parkhead I met Michael Kelly, the lord provost, who did so much to promote his city with the tag line "Glasgow's Miles Better" (I always read it as Glasgow Smiles Better). Across town, a visit to Ibrox always felt like being admitted to the inner sanctums of one of football's truly great institutions. Even if I did have one of my worst experiences in the game there.

On a cold Tuesday in December 1989, the Scottish champions played their English counterparts Arsenal in the Zenith Data Systems Challenge. The match was dubbed the championship of Britain. I was a guest in the boardroom as Arsenal won 2-1. At full-time, a business contact invited me into one of the corporate boxes for a drink. As I chatted away, a Rangers official took me aside. "Mr Duff, I'm afraid I'll have to ask you to leave." Apparently, the owner of the box was offended by my presence. He only welcomed "traditional" guests. Presumably, the entire box sat stone-faced when Mo Johnston scored Rangers' goal that night. By this time, I had become well versed in the nonsense of sectarianism. The Protestant boy who happened to love an 'Irish' club went back to the boardroom with a sad smile.

One great example of the worth of using the directors' box to cultivate vital friendships came just before kick-off when Rangers were our guests. Cecil informed me that he had received a phone call to say there was a bomb in the stadium. It was not possible to dismiss it as a hoax as the caller had given an IRA codeword. The threat appeared very real, and we had a potential disaster on our hands. Our choice was to evacuate more than 20,000 people onto the streets surrounding Easter Road, or sit it out and pray. The police match controller, for some unfathomable reason, looked at me to make the decision. I hadn't realised this was in my remit.

The first option had its problems; evacuation would likely cause panic, and a stampede might prove fatal. I was also worried that the hooligan firms that followed both teams would clash as we couldn't maintain segregation outside the stadium. The potential consequences of the second option, if there was really a bomb, were horrifying.

I was fortunate to have the second-most senior policeman in Edinburgh – off-duty Hector Clark – sat only a few feet from me. We were able to have a quick conversation, and I deferred to his judgement that the game should go ahead. I don't think I have ever been more frightened. Thankfully there was no bomb, and everyone went home safely. While I can't deny running a famous football club certainly gave my ego a stroke, I realised that day just what a responsibility I had taken on.

*

Before the Scottish Football Association moved its offices to Hampden Park, it was housed in a Victorian building in central Glasgow. There you would find Ernie Walker, the SFA's formidable-looking secretary. He sported a sergeant-major moustache and dressed like a proper gentleman. Polished shoes. Stiff upper lip, befitting of his military past.

Whether you were a player, manager or director, you feared a summons to Ernie's office. Invariably, whatever the misdemeanour, you'd be sent home with a dressing down, suspension or fine – possibly all three. It wasn't until the end of my tenure that I discovered that Ernie was an incredibly kind, modest and compassionate man. As chair of UEFA's Stadia Committee, he served the European game for 10 years. I know the terrible events that unfolded at Heysel in 1985 always weighed heavily on his mind.

Towards the end of every season, UEFA would write to all the clubs in their jurisdiction and offer them tickets to the European Cup final. In 1988, the final between PSV Eindhoven and Benfica was to be played in Stuttgart. We could request up to six tickets, and they would be allocated on a first-come, first served basis. I rushed to get an application in and was delighted to receive six golden final tickets. Along with Alex and Jim, I decided to treat our main sponsors, Frank and Robert Graham. This left one place spare. Luigi Palmero was a close friend who ran an Italian restaurant in West London. He loved his football. I invited him to make up our party.

We flew to Stuttgart the night before the match for a three-day break and booked into a swish city-centre hotel. We certainly enjoyed our first night in Stuttgart, coming down for breakfast in the morning still significantly the worse for wear. As I was loading up my plate with a continental breakfast, I became aware that we were in the company of some very esteemed guests. Unbeknown to us, the entire UEFA Executive Committee were booked into our hotel. Like pupils on a school trip who have snuck out to the pub, only to find their headteacher at the bar, we sat in silence, hoping our glassy eyes wouldn't give us away.

The stadium was around four miles from our hotel, and naively, we'd left it late to head out for the match. The traffic wasn't moving, and there was no way we'd be able to make it for kick-off by taxi. Parked outside the hotel, we noticed three coaches all clearly headed for the game. Several Dutch parties had rooms on our floor, and I assumed the coaches had been laid on for them. Well, we could pass as Dutch, couldn't we? The first coach door was open. The only person on the bus was the driver, who nodded to us as we walked to the back and took our seats.

As the coach filled up, my stomach sank. Rather than PSV fans, these coaches were for our UEFA friends from the breakfast bar. One of the last to clamber aboard was none other than Ernie Walker, who took a seat at the front next to UEFA's President Jacques Georges. The bus received a police escort as we sped to the stadium. We waved like the Queen to the joyous fans who packed the pavements anticipating the biggest night of their footballing lives. Perhaps we should have been a little quieter and blended in, but we'd enjoyed a beer or two in the hotel bar. I noticed Luigi speaking to a Scandinavian UEFA rep, bending his ear about all the ills of European football in his slurred, heavily Italian-accented English. Frank and Robert hid in their seats, occasionally popping up to see if anyone had noticed the six interlopers.

Alex was sure he'd committed career suicide. Jim, being on the Scottish League Committee, might have had a legitimate cause – at a push – to be on the coach. But, he too sat mortified next to Alex. As we approached the ground, the secretary of UEFA spoke over the public address system. "Enjoy the game, and please make sure to be back on the bus 40 minutes after the end of the match." With our return journey sorted, we enjoyed a tense game won by PSV on penalties.

As our tickets had been in the opposing stand to the UEFA delegation, we were late arriving back for the rapidly filling coaches. Ernie was already occupying his seat. There would be no way of avoiding detection this time. I edged along the aisle before our eyes locked. Without saying a word, Ernie nodded his head formally. Only after the last of our party had sat down did he turn and give me a little wink.

By the time our coach pulled up, thousands of delirious Dutch fans had gathered at the front of our hotel. Enjoying the moment, Frank, Robert and Luigi were only too happy to give the impression they were top UEFA execs. Then another coach arrived, and down the steps came the victorious PSV team with the European Cup. Now the three of them were masquerading as part of the winners' party, rubbing shoulders with Ronald Koeman and Guus Hiddink. It had never occurred to me that the hotel housing the UEFA officials would be the scene of the winning team's victory party. That night at the bar, we found ourselves next to the venerated UEFA President. When we recounted our story, he couldn't stop laughing.

*

Jim and I watched the final game of the 1987/88 season from the terrace behind the goal at Easter Road. We hugged those around us as Andy Goram scored with a mighty kick from his own penalty area in a 3-1 win over Morton. When I reflected on our first season, I judged it to be a qualified success. We finished sixth in the league, just shy of European qualification and three places better off than the previous campaign. We had taken Celtic to a replay in the Scottish Cup after a draw at Parkhead and had been unlucky when the sides met again, losing by the only goal.

After the collapse of the deal for David Platt, Alex had finally bought a forward, young Gareth Evans from Rotherham. At £60,000 and 20 years old, he was one for the future. Gareth made an immediate impact. His missus was an accomplished hairdresser and ensured that Gareth regularly had the best hair in the Scottish game. He would go on to have a long and distinguished Hibs career, even returning to Easter Road after hanging up his boots and taking on the role of caretaker-manager. England-born Gareth is a proper Leither and continues to work at the club, developing Hibs youngsters to this day. However, as Alex and the boys headed off for their summer holidays, it was clear where the team needed to improve. We had scored just 41 league goals, one fewer than we'd conceded. Only Motherwell and bottom club, Morton, had a worse record. We had to find a ready-made top-class striker. That was now my priority. It was a task I'd complete with or without the help of our manager. We could no longer wait.

Jim and I were very interested to read reports in the papers that Johan Cruyff, the Dutch master and new manager of Barcelona, wanted rid of Scotland's Stevie Archibald. I remembered Archie banging in the goals for Spurs before he moved on to Spain. Could we dare dream?

We quickly discovered that following a brief spell on loan at Blackburn Rovers, the striker had been told not to report back to the Camp Nou ahead of the new season. Barca were effectively paying Archie to stay away. When we made furtive enquiries about his availability, we couldn't believe our luck. They were willing to release him without a fee. In the opaque world of football transfers, it transpired that the signing rights for Archie belonged to an offshore company. Adding to the complexity, we were told to deal with a North London accountant, who had acted for the player since his Tottenham days.

The only reason he had not been snapped up on a free transfer by Liverpool, who were very keen, was that both he and his agent were demanding a signing-on fee. This would be equivalent to what we might have expected to pay in a regular transfer deal. The only difference was the destination of the money. Our initial secret meetings in London were with the agent alone. Jim would fly down to lead the negotiations. They were painfully long-winded.

We did our homework on Archie, asking Alex Ferguson, his former manager at Aberdeen, what kind of lad he was? The report soon came back. "Steve is a great, committed professional . . . but you'll need to install a chair in the manager's office with his name on it. He'll be in there every day, complaining or demanding something." With such a reputation, I could and perhaps should have shown caution. But once we got to meet Archie in person, I found him an amusing and intelligent character, who I quickly became very fond of.

If lining up the deal had been taxing, the real challenge was convincing our manager to agree. "I don't want him," was Alex's blunt response when we put it to him. "All right, Alex, give me a list of strikers you do want," I replied. He offered no names and, reluctantly, conceded that the player should be signed. However, I don't think Alex ever really clicked with Archie, believing (correctly) that we had foisted the forward on him.

The fee eventually agreed was £350,000. Archie insisted he would only sign if he became the top earner at the club above John Collins and Andy Goram. It was always a delicate balancing act agreeing to a new signing's wage demands when they exceeded what our existing star players were on. Most footballers aren't shy about telling the chairman – or their teammates – what they think they're worth. By now, however, my heart was set on Archie. I had seen him play many, many times and knew he was different class. I was willing to pay to get the best and risk any friction caused in the dressing room. We agreed on a salary that was precisely £1 more a week than that of Collins and Goram.

To put things in context, Barcelona signed Archie from Spurs for £1.2 million as a replacement for Diego Maradona. In Catalonia, he won La Liga and reached a European Cup final. Before then, during his time at White Hart Lane, he had scored 77 goals in fewer than 200 games. He was also capped 27 times by Scotland, playing at both the 1982 and 1986 World Cups. In my book, this was a great piece of business. We were getting a bargain.

We had finally delivered the big-name forward the club so desperately needed. Our fans, and Scottish football, were absolutely buzzing at the prospect of Archie wearing the green and white in the coming campaign.

SIX

HIGH-FLYING

THE FIXTURE LIST for the new 1988/89 season was not kind. After our first home game against Motherwell, which we won 1-0, we had to play Rangers at Ibrox, Hearts at home, and then travel to Aberdeen and Dundee United. Although we scored only once in this block of fixtures, we remained unbeaten. I was not too concerned about the lack of goals. I had come to understand that, no matter how many forwards we signed, the way Alex set us up, we were never going to be free-scoring. But we would be bloody hard to beat.

Archie scored twice on his debut for us, a League Cup tie against Stranraer at Easter Road. I was convinced – one way or another – we were now on a march that would lead us to Europe.

On the afternoon of 31 August, 1988, I was in Edinburgh looking forward to a League Cup quarter-final against Aberdeen. We were at home, and although at the time, the Dons were the only team in Scotland keeping some sort of pace with the Old Firm, we believed we could win. With the game evenly poised at 1-1 and only a few minutes remaining, Gareth Evans was played through. As he raced forward and steadied himself to score a potential winner, Dons keeper Theo Snelders charged from his line and cleaned Gareth out, handling the ball outside of his box for good measure. In today's game, the Dutchman would have been dismissed without question – honestly, the challenge was worthy of two red cards. In 1988, however, the referee somehow saw fit to only show a yellow. Suffice to say, the Easter Road faithful, complete with hand gestures, did not agree. With Snelders – who'd been having a blinder – saving Paul Kane's resulting free-kick, the game swung in their favour. In a terrible miscarriage of footballing justice, Aberdeen scored an extra-time winner.

It is one of my faults that I think good losers are born losers. Nevertheless, I have always aspired to be gracious in defeat and show good manners. Or perhaps more accurately, I wanted to try. After the game, at the bottom of the stairs leading up from the tunnel to the directors' box, I was chatting to David Brown, our welcoming ambassador at Easter Road. Nearby, on the half landing, was Aberdeen director (and one-time Manchester United full-back), Ian Donald, loudly praising Snelders to a member of his official party. Unlike the Aberdeen goalie, I saw red. Ian and I engaged in a public shouting match where I let myself down badly. The only other time I really lost it was when I questioned the referee's parentage to his face when Danny Lennon's leg was broken. Mr Donald, much water has passed under our bridges since that night, but I belatedly apologise. Theo Snelders, however, you remain for ever unforgiven.

*

The need to travel up and down Scotland with the team on top of commuting between London, Wiltshire and Edinburgh proved challenging for me, particularly as I had developed a severe fear of flying. For many years, it meant a restriction on family holidays abroad, and trips from London were made either in the car or by train. I particularly loved the Caledonian Sleeper.

But in my early weeks as chairman, I forced myself to take the London to Edinburgh shuttle flight. I would endure an hour of abject terror, knowing the misery of a return journey was only a day or two away.

As a curative therapy, I decided I would learn to fly an aircraft. Turnhouse Airport was a busy little hub, accommodating two flying clubs and an RAF base where pilots trained. There were private planes on the apron too. Kwik Fit chairman Tom Farmer was the owner of one. I remember hearing that on occasion Sir Tom would kindly lay on his jet for members of the Scottish Catholic church.

I joined the Turnhouse Flying Club, and on Saturday mornings took to the air to perform circuits and practise landing and take-off. The exercise was called touch and go – an appropriate description of how my stomach felt in those early lessons. With time I came to love flying. Sometimes, if we were playing at Aberdeen, I would pilot myself up for the game and then come back at night, seeing the whole of Scotland, with the lights of the major towns, below me. It was inspirational.

The Flying Club had a bar and car park on the Cammo side of the airport. It had fallen into financial problems. I was asked if I would be interested in buying it and decided to make an offer. All three bids came from existing Turnhouse patrons. We each had to prepare a presentation on how we would run the club, and the other members would vote on the preferred purchaser. My presentation did the trick. Inadvertently I had become not just the Hibs chairman but a fully-fledged Edinburgh businessman. The *Evening News* had my picture taken, with me stood beside a small Cessna 150 aeroplane, ready to go on a jolly.

Sadly, as the years went by, both the other bidders died in air accidents. One crashed into Hill of Beath, with the other coming down close by. I had some near misses, too. Single-engine flying is dangerous, and I've long since hung up my pilot's headset.

There was one occasion that I flew to a game at Dens Park, Dundee. Unbeknown to me, the local airport closed early in winter. There was no problem when I flew in, but after the game, the airfield was deserted. In a moment of absolute reckless madness, I decided to take off with only the lights of my aircraft to guide me through the pitch dark. I taxied slowly down the length of the runway to ensure there was nothing parked on it. Satisfied, I turned and headed full speed the other way, before rotating and lifting into the night sky. Had I been caught, I would have been deservedly grounded for ever. Worse, I could have crashed, and the crisis that later engulfed Hibernian Football Club would have played out very differently.

*

It did not take long for Fergie's prediction about Steve Archibald to come true. Archie's relationship with our manager, which started badly, soon became fraught. The pair would regularly clash over team selection and Alex's approach to the game. Archie was as good as any player in the league, and at this stage of his career, he knew it. I think winding Alex up almost became a bit of a game for him. Yet despite his sizeable ego, Archie set a great example in training and on the park. Our young players idolised him, and he was generous with his time and advice.

While most of the players drove modest cars – Paul Kane would give several of the boys a lift to training in his Lada – Archie bought himself a Rolls-Royce. To ensure there was no doubt over its owner, the number plate, SA1, heralded the occupant. I always wondered why that plate did not belong to the South African ambassador. It came as no real surprise that Archie gravitated towards the more outgoing – some might say naughty – members of the squad. He struck up a firm friendship with Andy Goram.

One Friday night, after I had been to dinner at Cosmo's, I went on for a late-night drink. Not that many establishments stay open in Edinburgh past midnight, but one of the most popular was a cocktail bar, situated in a basement just off George Street, called Charlie Parker's. I ordered a drink and chatted with some regulars I knew. Then I became aware of some boyish giggling emanating from behind me. Upon investigation, I found Archie and Andy hiding from me ducked down on the business side of the bar. They'd sought refuge there when they clocked me coming down the stairs. Archie was not much of a drinker and liked orange juice. But occasionally, at his leisure, he would add vodka to his preferred tipple. I should explain, at this point, it was now the early hours of Saturday morning, and the pair would be starting for us in a game at Easter Road later that afternoon.

When, in the twilight of his career, George Best played for Hibs, he would fly up from London on the morning of the match. The management could never actually be sure he was coming. Even once he'd made it to Edinburgh, they'd have to delay picking their starting XI. En route to Easter Road, George would visit a small bar in the West End of the city for a drink or two as part of his pre-match preparation. In the end, Cecil Graham was dispatched to collect him off the plane. Such was George's otherworldly talent – no matter what state he arrived in – he would always be the best player on the park.

The prospect of seeing a genuine footballing icon drew bumper crowds, and the management accordingly afforded George special treatment. I remember in one of the 25 precious appearances he made for Hibs, George preparing to take a freekick in front of the Rangers fans. As he bent down to place the ball on the turf, a beer can was lobbed at him from the terraces. George being George, he picked it up, cracked it open and took a mighty swig – before whipping in an inch-perfect cross. Andy and Steve were not George Best. But they had some of his aura about them.

There was always the fear that some awful press article might appear, complete with photos of our players falling out of a pub ahead of a big game. I probably worried unnecessarily. Unlike their counterparts south of the border, the Scottish press, in general, turned away from the bad behaviour of the nation's footballing heroes. On a later date, after an international match, I witnessed a Scottish player (who did not play for Hibs) taking a line of cocaine in the toilet. Jim Kean, of the *Daily Record*, was washing his hands in the gents at the time. Although he must have seen what was happening, no front-page 'exclusive' of this personal habit was ever printed.

Back at Charlie Parker's, I pondered what to say to Archibald and Goram when suddenly I heard more familiar voices coming our way. It was Alex and Peter, who were obviously enjoying their own night out. Without thinking – and in line with every good farce ever written – I panicked and joined the players behind the bar. There the Hibs chairman and two-star players hid from the club's manager and his assistant. Alex and Peter did not stay long, and we got away undiscovered.

Later that afternoon, Goram played superbly and ended the game with another of his clean sheets. After the match, I went up to the super executive room. Man of the Match? Steve Archibald, who gave me a wink as he took the bottle of champagne.

Although I was not much older than most of the boys, they showed me great respect. I can't say I always merited it. Some club staff would call me Mr Duff, others David, but the players insisted on "chairman". They were always up for a joke and happy to include me in their fun. Those moments sharing a laugh with the boys are the memories I cherish most, although I made sure to never again have a Friday night drink at Charlie Parker's. And, hopefully, nor did the players.

I should stress not all the boys were 'Champagne Charlies'. Gordon Rae, our skipper, was the archetypal family man.

Gordon, an uncompromising centre-back, came to Hibs in 1975 as a youth player and stayed with the club for 15 years. He once chillingly disclosed his method for dealing with flashy forwards who tried to embarrass him with flicks and tricks; "Well, I play keepy-uppy wi' the strikers."

In the new season, it was brought to my attention that Gordon was due a testimonial. I endorsed the idea immediately. Ironically, loyal players can lose out financially. This is because the re-signing fee at the end of a contract is less than they could expect to receive upon joining a new club. As compensation, a testimonial year provided a lump sum, as well as the honour of being recognised by the club they served.

The highlight of a player's testimonial year is the testimonial match. However, many other events are organised, and the formal dinner represents another source of well-deserved funds. A special testimonial committee is formed, usually containing a club director, local businessmen and fans. While the club throws its resources behind the events, it does not interfere with the organisation.

Gordon's dinner included a performance by The Proclaimers, the club's most famous fans. There were many dignitaries and local businessmen all happy to contribute a good amount. Jockey, Jonjo O'Neill, who had just recovered from cancer, was one of several stars from the wider sporting world to attend.

For the testimonial match, we again deployed the ace up our sleeve. Martin asked Alex Ferguson if Manchester United would come up to Easter Road. Such was Fergie's regard for big Gordon he immediately agreed. The players were excited, in particular, our winger, Joe Tortolano. Joe had always dreamed of playing in a match against his hero Gordon Strachan.

Early in the game, Joe put in a tackle that threatened to dismember Strachan. The regular practice in a match like this would be for the referee to immediately demand the player be substituted, which Alex Miller no doubt would have done. Instead, the country's top ref George Smith sent Joe off, leaving Gordon Rae a team of 10 men to play out the remaining 84 minutes of his testimonial. United won the match 3-0.

There was a marvellous dinner after the game; I am sure the speeches touched Gordon and created memories for him and his family to cherish. A few years after my Hibs days, I bumped into Gordon in Tesco, and we had the chance to talk about his career. He was nothing but humble. Few men have served Hibernian Football Club with such distinction.

SEVEN

EDINBURGH HIBERNIAN PLC

I WAS ONCE asked during a BBC *Sportscene* interview if I was trying to compete with Celtic and Rangers. Too bloody right I was. I wanted Hibs to win trophies, and the Old Firm were the teams to beat. But, unlike them, I could never put 50,000 bums on seats at Easter Road, so I had to find another way. Today, clubs create many income streams with partnerships across the world, but back then, a club's financial health was near totally aligned to what happened on the pitch. In Scotland, the home club keeps all the income generated from league games – meaning a drop in attendances, poor sponsorships or, at worst, relegation was potentially ruinous.

From day one, I intended to float the club. I believed this would be the paradigm shift that would enable us to break the Glasgow duopoly. There were three markets on the London Stock Exchange, and I aimed to take Hibs onto the Third Market, which dealt with smaller companies. I wanted us to list as a property business. We had a near six-acre stadium and a further six acres of development land, so we fitted that bill.

My plan was reasonably straightforward: fortify the club with solid property assets that produced a guaranteed profit, thereby making the volatile football income less crucial. I knew from acting for INOCO that David Rowland had some diverse property assets in Scotland, which he promised to offer to us. It was a mixed commercial bundle that included, for example, the office block down the road at Meadowbank, where the tenant was the UK government who used it to house the tax office.

Investing in property was particularly attractive, as it would not require us to hire a vast number of new staff or leave Hibs responsible for providing a raft of services beyond football. Our only task would be to find tenants. Given the quality of the properties Rowland proposed to put our way, that would be easy. A stable rental income would be transformative for the club. We estimated it would effectively double our revenue, which, in turn, would allow us to buy better players for the first team.

A further advantage of diversifying into commercial properties was that the rent a property commands determines its capital value. Therefore if we increased the rent, having acquired the property, we would also then be able to sell it in the future for a significant profit.

Rowland agreed to sell his Scottish properties to Hibs if the flotation was successful. From his point of view, he would end up owning a big chunk of the club and would benefit financially as both the seller and purchaser of the properties. If this secured a fiscally strong Hibernian, that was fine by me.

Immediately upon becoming chairman, I had set about implementing my plan for the flotation. I attended daily meetings with our accountants (Deloitte Haskins & Sells) and lawyers, knocking the club into shape. To float Hibernian, I required three years of good company accounts. But the books of the Kenny Waugh era were not acceptable to the stock exchange, so some historical investigation was necessary.

I had problems verifying gate income, as the collection of cash and paperwork did not tally. The turnstile clicked over each time a fan went through, and the numbers admitted to the ground needed to match the cash banked. There was also a scandal brewing over work conducted on the main enclosure predating my time. A director on Waugh's Hibs board had been simultaneously a director of Tensa, the company awarded the contract to carry out these ground improvements. Tensa had gone into receivership before completing the work, and alleged discrepancies between the amount paid to Tensa and the amount claimed in an application to the Football Grounds Improvement Trust eventually resulted in criminal proceedings.

We pushed ahead, managing to overcome many of the problems, and within six weeks looked on course for the flotation. I spoke with potential investors, and there was no shortage of institutions that wanted a stake in a David Rowland company.

As well as making mistakes of my own during my tenure at Hibs, I was also the victim of some awful bad luck. On Monday, 19 October, 1987, just two weeks before I was due to launch the flotation, I met with Rowland and the accountants. We sat in the office and watched the world fall apart. This date will for ever be known as Black Monday, the day the stock exchange crashed. You could no longer float a rubber duck in a bath. I had no option but to shelve the plan, ready to try again – I hoped – once the economy rebounded.

A year on from this abortive attempt, Rowland and I agreed that the market was unlikely to recover sufficiently to make the flotation work in the way we'd originally planned. Britain was moving towards recession, and the years ahead looked lean. There was nothing to be gained by delaying any further.

Between us, we reformulated the plan. The flotation would see us sell half the stock in the newly formed public company. But instead of offering the majority of these shares to fans and small shareholders, we would now aim for them to own 40% while placing 60% with financial institutions. As we had invested heavily in the team, we agreed that the purchase of Rowland's Scottish properties would be financed somewhere down the line with a second share issue. By then, all being well, the club would have made progress, and the stock market would be resurgent. I worked non-stop to create a document that would meet the strict requirements of the stock exchange. Our lawyers and accountants were in London, so the bulk of the work was done there. John Kerr of Strathern & Blair and his partners represented our interests in Edinburgh, and they proved to be more competent and hard-working than the London advisers.

Flotation requires a meticulous process of verification. The stock exchange document is scrutinised line by line to prove every single word is factual. Having created a document full of accurate accounting and a very tight plan for our future, the most daunting job of all remained. We still had to sell the financial plan to the institutions.

Although the people we hoped might be prospective buyers knew Rowland and his reputation for success, they would not buy shares on that alone. They had shareholders, pension funds and bank managers of their own to satisfy. Rowland arranged meetings with interested parties both in the City of London and around Charlotte Square in Edinburgh. It was my job to deliver the sales pitch. I had to convince top fund managers and investment specialists that Hibs was a premier league financial investment.

I could envisage a future for Britain's biggest football clubs as diverse businesses providing multiple services to their fans and significant community work. Games would take place in modern stadiums televised around the globe. Buying into Hibs was buying into this vision. Each institution we courted to invest in the club was different, with a strategy and style of its own. Sometimes I'd be presenting to a formal boardroom packed with senior executives in pinstripe suits. On other occasions, it involved a friendly chat over a cup of tea and a Jammie Dodger.

After three intense days of meetings, where I buzzed between the financial capitals of England and Scotland, one by one the institutions committed to investing in Hibs. Ivory & Sime, an Edinburgh fund of international repute run by Allan Munro, were particularly keen. Allan had been a Hibs fanatic since he was a boy, and David Rowland loved the idea of presenting to a Hibs fan and saw Munro as an asset in our plans going forward. Allan soon became a regular guest in the directors' box on Easter Road match days.

We had structured the corporate plan so that we would float a new company called Edinburgh Hibernian PLC. The Hibernian Football Club Limited was a subsidiary of the new public limited company. Our remaining task was to sell the other 40% of shares on offer to the fans. Their motivation was owning a piece of the club they loved rather than any desire to receive a dividend. They were happy to frame the share certificate and put it on their mantelpiece. I know some fans still have their Edinburgh Hibernian PLC share certificate to this day.

In the early months of the 1988/89 season – thanks to Archie's arrival – our gate numbers had risen. But were there enough fans to take up the share offer? Jim Gray was a master at setting up meetings with individuals in the Edinburgh business community who might be interested. Some of those we contacted jumped at the chance. A few, like Kwik Fit supremo Tom Farmer, never returned Jim's calls.

We explained the share offer in consecutive match programmes. We even commissioned a pioneering television advert featuring match-going Hibs fans as extras. More than 300 turned up to give their time for free, even though the filming required them to miss a day's work. Alex and the players also took part, and Jim and I even got in on the act. Ian St John narrated the advert, which you can still find out there on YouTube. The camera pans along the Easter Road bench, while 'The Saint' points out that rather than John Collins or Alex Miller being the most important people at Easter Road, "It's you. Hibs fans." Alongside the famous footballing faces occupying the dugout, we then see the somewhat-less-svelte figure of a middle-aged supporter wearing full kit, Hibs bobble hat and a cheeky smile. The fan begins to limber up pitch-side, before being subbed on in a fictional match. The supporter in question was comedian and real-life Hibs fan, Gary Dennis.

As we approached 3 October, 1988, our launch date, I was getting daily updates on the number of applications received. We were significantly short of our target. While shares were selling well, we didn't have enough fans willing to take up the 40% we'd earmarked for them. I ramped up the publicity and went on breakfast TV, to be interviewed by Derek Jameson. While I tried to put on a brave face for the cameras, this was a facade. I was distraught. The problem was, if we were undersubscribed at the launch, the share price would immediately drop. Whereas oversubscription would see the price rise. An increase was essential for the institutions that had invested. It would be the difference between success and failure. Also, even if fans weren't in it for a quick profit, we hoped they'd see the shares they'd bought at 55 pence trading immediately for a good bit more.

Rowland kept telling me not to worry and to keep pushing the message. I took to the radio and toured our supporters' clubs. With days to go, as a result of these efforts, the picture had improved. But we had still received applications for around only two-thirds of the shares on offer. Then a miracle happened. A raft of applications came in for large amounts of shares. There is always a last-minute rush, but this wildly exceeded my expectations. By the closing day, somehow, we were now oversubscribed. The quoted price exceeded the offer price. Someone had answered my prayers. Hibernian became the first team in Scotland to float, and behind Tottenham Hotspur, only the second in Britain.

In the jubilation of success, however, I had a nagging doubt about those late applications. Something felt off. If any major shareholder in the company was attempting to manipulate the share price by concealment, it would be a matter for the authorities. When I looked at where the applications came from, they were from nominee accounts from overseas banks. There was no easy way of knowing who the real owners were. I wanted to know if David Rowland could shed any light on the matter.

Rowland was in Monaco. He owned a stunning flat in the principality overlooking his favourite spot, the famous nightclub, Jimmy'z. He also had an £11 million yacht which cost £1 million a year to service. If you wanted to live in this community, it seemed compulsory to flaunt your wealth. When I asked for a meeting to discuss the flotation 'miracle', Rowland invited me to Monaco for the weekend. He booked my flight on Air France, where I found myself seated in Club Class, eating hot pain au chocolat and exotic fruit for breakfast.

Rowland met me at the airport, and we drove to his yacht in Antibes. From there, we sailed to Monte Carlo. Unexpectedly, when we arrived, I found Sheila was there. She stayed for the rest of the weekend, and we both slept on the boat with the crew. In the evening, we met David for dinner, where he introduced me to the Barclay brothers. The conversation quickly turned to business. These billionaire twins were operating at the highest level of international commerce. They owned a massive hotel group and were into just about every sector of commercial activity. They were stars in that world. If the introduction was an attempt to impress me, it worked. I felt I was discussing my ambitions with business royalty.

The next day, the captain of our temporary home took us out in the speedboat that hung from the yacht's rear, and we swam in the perfect sea. In the evening, we drank champagne at Jimmy'z. It was intoxicating. When I was back at the airport the following morning, I realised I had not spent a moment alone with Rowland. All my questions remained unanswered, and the identities of those late buyers who had 'saved' the flotation remained opaque. But I never forgot about those accounts, and it gnawed away at me. I could not have known at that time the vital part they would later play in saving Hibs from extinction.

EIGHT

MY PAST AND A SONG

NELLIE FOX LIVED on the Canongate. She was known by everybody and watched the world go by from her first-floor window. Nellie was the best storyteller I ever met and could point out a passer-by and recount facts about their family history even they didn't know. I loved visiting her and hearing those incredible tales.

I am proud to say that Nellie Fox was my grandmother. As a teenager, visiting her became part of my Easter Road matchday routine. I would pop in for a legendary Nellie Fox lunch and often need to run to make kick-off, having lost track of time after being enraptured by her stories. She loved to watch me walk down the Canongate wrapped in Hibs colours. What a joy it was, years later, to have my grandmother in the directors' box at Easter Road.

She was a woman who did not keep possessions. If you brought something to her, the next visitor would undoubtedly leave with it, your gift having been lovingly passed on. In wanting nothing, she was rarely intimidated, and she mixed easily with the dignitaries in the boardroom. I suspect she recounted many stories from the directors' box to others. And she probably knew many hidden secrets about those she met.

One of Nellie's favourite days of the year was when royalty arrived in Edinburgh. When taking residence at Holyrood Palace, royal visitors would be driven down Nellie's road in a vast convoy. My grandmother would always be at her window waving.

One morning a letter arrived at Easter Road, inviting me to Her Majesty's annual garden party. There weren't too many royalists at Hibernian. But I had no hesitation in accepting the invite, knowing what it would mean to my granny. I only wish I could have smuggled her in with me. A trip to Moss Bros ensured I was decked out in the correct attire. The party itself was conducted in bright sunshine. The Queen, the Duke of Edinburgh, Prince Andrew and Princess Anne each took a corner of the garden. Neat lines like at a theme park would form before them as guests queued for a brief chat with their Windsor of choice.

I opted for Princess Anne, and, after a short time, she greeted me. It was protocol to introduce myself and explain what I did. The Princess is patron of the Scottish Rugby Union; she has a good knowledge of sport in general, and I enjoyed her company. She has always been my favourite royal.

After the garden party, I decided to walk into town and, as I strolled past her window, there was Nellie, waving down at the toff in formal dress. Even now, many years later and long after my grandmother passed, I still feel her presence whenever I'm in Edinburgh.

When I was born, I was taken back from Elsie Inglis Hospital to a flat above a butcher's shop in Bonnington Road. It was pretty rudimentary accommodation where we shared an outdoor toilet. My father had been denied an education because of the Second World War. And like so many of his generation, providing his children with the best schooling possible became an obsession for him. I already had an older brother and sister and, over time, would be joined by a younger brother and sister too. My paternal grandfather died just before I was born. He had a close attachment to my elder brother, who is six years my senior. My dad had vowed on his father's deathbed to give him the education he had been deprived.

My father was a fireman based in Leith. When I was four, he accepted an opportunity to become a bus driver earning a bit more money. As a result, we were able to move to Perth. Dad later found his true calling as a superb salesman of fire-safety equipment. By dint of his effort, our family was transported from abject poverty to middle-class comfort. Following Dad's work, we moved to England, first to Yorkshire and then to Bromley, where I spent my formative years.

My big brother was and is a genius. This made my father's task of giving him the best education and honouring his promise significantly easier. His ability to attain straight As in all he did set an impossible benchmark for the rest of us. It felt as if we could never achieve enough. This made me a rebel at school, and I certainly underachieved before leaving aged 15. I wanted to be a film cameraman and worked for a new company called World Microfilms, in Warren Street, London. It was hard graft for low pay, and I soon realised leaving education had been a mistake. Dad's job now took the family back to Scotland, so I returned to school in Edinburgh, courtesy of a visionary headmaster, who offered me a second chance.

From there, I went to teacher training college in Doncaster. I became president of the students' union and later vice-chair of Sheffield Students. I met many future Labour politicians who shaped my politics for life and sparked my desire to change paths and work in the law. Qualifying as a solicitor, and being in training for four years, was the biggest challenge of my life, and I prized the qualification I earned. I owe much to the mother of my children, who supported me in the last two years of training. By the start of the 1980s, I was a bit of an enigma, a socialist, a

Thatcherite, and a yuppie. The first house I speculatively bought was in Munster Road, Fulham, and was something called a "part possession". This meant a sitting tenant was living on the ground floor. The house was not converted, so I did not have my own front door. To reach the upstairs involved walking through the tenant's home to access an open flight of stairs. I exchanged contracts to purchase the freehold of the house for £12,000 on a 100% mortgage from Barclays Bank. But before completion, a developer client offered me £18,000 for the contract, and I readily agreed to sell. I made a £6,000 profit without even completing the transaction. It represented two years of my solicitor's training salary. I was off to the races.

The bank was prepared to lend again. I bought, sold and let properties all over the borough – definitely more Thatcherite than socialist at this point. This is how I started as a property speculator and conveyancer – I became very knowledgeable in the field. When I qualified as a solicitor and moved from London to Marlborough, I acted for the Ramsbury Building Society. Over time, they amalgamated with Western County, becoming the West of England Building Society and later the Portland Building Society. A new chief executive, Ken Culley, was brought in from Chester. We struck up a friendship playing rugby together at Marlborough. Ken went on to have a stellar career, rising to the chair of the Building Societies Association. Before that, however, he and I invested in property together. He enabled me to acquire multiple mortgages and played a significant part in building my wealth.

Playing rugby brought me into contact with other brokers, who also provided me with mortgages. I would sign blank application forms for some financial advisers who would submit them directly to the institution on my behalf, adding whatever information they needed. This was a routine practice at the time for people buying multiple properties. Later, it would come to have dire personal consequences.

I rented out the properties I bought, and the rents paid the mortgages. Briefly, it seemed under Thatcher, people like me were making inroads into the hereditary class system for the first time. The property market kept rising, and on paper, I became ever richer. When I arrived at Hibs in 1987, I was widely described as a "millionaire". The equity in my properties proved that to be true. But I have always said that you are only as rich as your liquidity, the amount in your pocket. The 1980s were littered with "millionaires" who actually had no cash.

*

By the 1988/89 season, I had a legal firm with four branches to run, a property business, and was chairman of the football club I loved. I would soon add to that list a failing leisure company. Only in retrospect do I see that it was too much. At the time, I was living the dream and felt I was invincible. People saw me as a wildly successful entrepreneur and would ask my advice on matters I knew nothing about. Shame on me – I would give it to them anyway. Jim Kean at the *Daily Record* would ask me about rumours in English football, and I was "the source" behind many a story.

I even fancied myself as a record producer and, to this aim, decided Hibernian Football Club needed an anthem. In the past, most Scottish football songs had served as the soundtrack to the national team's latest World Cup embarrassment. I wanted ours to be a rallying cry that Hibs supporters could feel proud of and belt out before matches. I approached two singer-songwriters I was friendly with to help, Colin Chisholm and Brian Spence. They had enjoyed success a few years before in a band called Bilbo Baggins. Colin was a committed Jambo, while Brian is a Hibee. The song was written and recorded in London.

They didn't let me down, and we produced what I think is still one of the best football songs ever written. 'Hibs Heroes' was a bit of a forerunner to the likes of 'Don't Come Home Too Soon'. It encapsulates what the club means to its fans and the community. If you look the song up on YouTube, you will find this comment from Ashley Carter: "This was played today at my grandad's funeral service. He was a great Hibs fan. Thanks, Hibs, for being great. The lyrics mean a lot to us personally." It warms my heart that, after three decades, the song still touches Hibs supporters in this way.

Colin was also partly responsible for another great addition to the Hibernian family: our very own club greyhound. Colin had a kennel out by the airport. Occasionally I would have a night out with him, watching the races at Powderhall Stadium. I ended up buying one of his dogs which had not yet been given a racing name. I decided to run a competition in the matchday programme where fans could send in their suggestions. The winning entry would be rewarded with a place in the directors' box and boardroom hospitality for a game later in the season. We were inundated with hilarious potential names for our greyhound. Some were far too rude to print and therefore could not be considered. My favourite, for obvious reasons, was Heart-beater, but Jim got the casting vote and plumped for Cabbage and Ribs. I think a fair few Hibees – and some of the players – won a bob or two backing Cabbage and Ribs. Mind you, I still reckon Mickey Weir could have beaten him over 10 yards.

To put 'Hibs Heroes' out, I formed my own record label, Duff Records. The sleeve for the freshly cut vinyl was green, of course. Late one night, when the record was ready, I picked up a dozen boxes from the pressers in Islington. I sent copies to Radio Forth and Radio Scotland, arranging for it to be sold in Edinburgh record shops. It did well in Scotland and was Edinburgh's number one single for a while. We played the song at all the home games, and it seems to have withstood the test of time. It's even now on Spotify. 'Hibs Heroes' was recently refreshed by the Edinburgh band Retro Video Club. Their frontman Liam Allison performed a sterling live rendition on the Easter Road pitch before the first derby of 2022. I wish I'd been there to see it.

It saddens me that on the back of Wallace Mercer's takeover bid, Brian Spence would say some uncharitable things about my time at the club. I hope if he reads this, he'll finally have the full facts of what happened.

Around the time the record was released, I became aware that one of the current 'Hibs Heroes' was in some serious trouble in his private life. Andy Goram – like many of our players at the time – was a big gambler. He saw everything and anything as a chance to have a flutter. One time, I foolishly boasted about my pedigree as a decent long-distance runner within earshot of our goalie. Immediately, the players demanded a race with me, with Andy running a book. My pride kicked in, and despite being past my athletic prime, I somehow agreed to take them on in a 10k around Arthur's Seat.

To make it a real contest, I was to receive a mile head start. I began to train in earnest. Luckily for me, one of the players mentioned the upcoming showdown to Alex Miller. Alex asked Jim Gray to put a stop to the whole thing before I could humiliate myself or worse. As Jim tactfully explained, the prospect of the club's chairman being carried off Edinburgh's iconic peak – having suffered a heart attack while engaged in a mad wager with his own players – perhaps wasn't in keeping with the fine traditions of Hibernian.

While bets like these were a bit of fun, the combination of money and free afternoons could lead some of the lads down horribly destructive paths. One day, Andy came to Jim Gray in a distressed state. He had run up debts with some Glasgow gangsters who were now threatening to break his hands. A particularly frightening prospect for a goalkeeper. Andy refused to take our advice and go to the police. He was determined to both honour his debt and keep his hands in working order.

Nobody wanted the story to get out. As well as Andy's welfare, we had to consider the potential adverse publicity for the club. I negotiated with the gangsters and agreed on a repayment package with them.

It seems incredible now, but in those days, players were paid weekly in cash. The mad practice was a throwback to football's working-class roots. We agreed with Andy that we would deduct an amount from his wages until the debt was paid off. The gangsters promised never to contact Andy again and swore to me that they would not offer credit to any other Hibs player. I very much doubt they were as good as their word.

It was apparent that Andy's living situation was problematic. Andy Roxburgh had played a crucial role in convincing him to sign for Hibs. The then-Scotland manager had told Andy that a move north of the border would enhance his prospects for the national team. Andy was so determined to be Scotland's number 1, he agreed to the transfer before he'd consulted his wife. She decided she didn't want to relocate from Lancashire with their young son, and I know the end of their marriage broke Andy's heart.

Andy was beloved at the club, and everyone who could see he was spiralling out of control wanted to help him. In the end, the intervention Andy really needed came inadvertently from Hearts. A close friend called Alison lived a few streets from Easter Road and worked in the Tynecastle corporate lounge. She agreed to take Andy as a lodger, and so it was that our goalkeeper came to be cared for by a Heart of Midlothian employee. From then on, ahead of the Edinburgh derby Andy would always pop into the Tynecastle lounge to say hello to his landlady. Alison told me this created much mirth among those she was entertaining.

In time, Andy moved from Alison's house to live with his new girlfriend. I would often ask him if he was okay, and he would always say "yes". The struggles Andy faced with addiction throughout the rest of his life have been well documented. I wish, looking back, that we had been more knowledgeable about player well-being and could have helped him more than we did. This is an area of the game that thankfully has improved beyond recognition since my time. Despite these difficulties, Andy was the best keeper in Scotland. He was immense for the morale and confidence of the team and a true Hibernian great.

*

A third of the way into the 1988/89 season, it was time for our first visit to Tynecastle, where we had not won for a decade. The home Hearts jinx had been broken – now could we bury the away one?

On arrival on 12 November, 1988, I saw Alison and chatted with her. I was later told that Wallace Mercer had spotted us and typically thought I was fraternising with his staff to wind him up. His mood did not improve from there. Derby hostilities began in the tunnel before a ball was kicked. Our physio Stuart Collie was accused of elbowing Hearts captain Gary Mackay. Stuart had been buffeted by the heavy-handed Hearts stewards and, in the stramash that ensued, caught Mackay inadvertently.

Once the game started, Paul Kane gave us the early advantage with a towering header. Our jubilation did not last long. Only 25 minutes into the first half, Gordon Rae was red-carded for two awful tackles. It would have to be backs-to-the-wall football for the rest of the match. Having watched our captain trudge off, we almost lost Archie too. During half-time, the striker barricaded himself in the Tynecastle toilets and demanded to be taken off. To be fair to Archie, the Hearts players had been kicking lumps out of him all afternoon. Adding to his dismay, Alex now instructed him to retreat behind the ball rather than pushing for a second goal to kill the game. Thankfully, appealing to Archie's testicular fortitude, our manager managed to talk him around.

Deep into the second half, with darkness descending over the ground, the boys clung to the lead, with Andy Goram making a string of brilliant saves. I was beginning to believe. Then with seven minutes to play, Archie latched on to an acrobatic Kano clearance and tore away from the Hearts defence. From the edge of the box, our star signing unleashed a low drive into the bottom corner beyond Henry Smith's despairing dive. The Hibs fans were stood behind that goal, and the scenes were joyous pandemonium. Hearts pulled one back in injury time, which was a mere consolation. Edinburgh was painted green and white that night.

NINE

SINGING THE AVON INNS BLUES

MARTIN LONGMAN WAS a Bristol businessman. I did not know him, but he was about to change my life. Before Black Monday, Martin spotted a hotel for sale near Weston-super-Mare. Given the very reasonable asking price, Martin believed he could flip it for a handsome return.

I do not know how he'd made David Rowland's acquaintance, but the pair agreed on a partnership to finance the purchase. David Rowland loved to make a profit, and, apparently, this deal made him a vast one. Martin Longman then explained he could repeat the trick, so Rowland offered him a line of credit to buy leisure businesses. Longman quickly put together a whole diverse package of hotels, pubs, clubs and restaurants, all in the West Country. All beyond his area of expertise.

After the 'successful' flotation of Hibernian, I set about reviewing prospective commercial properties owned by Rowland for the club to invest in. Under our agreement, Rowland was to help us finance these deals, which, in turn, would secure increased revenues for Hibs. I studied the leases, subleases and the predicted future rents of these potential purchases. I was determined to ensure stability for those who had invested in the club.

In the rippling shockwaves caused by the stock market crash, Longman's leisure empire spectacularly imploded. Any publican will tell you that you must always pay your brewery bill. Longman had failed to do this, and the brewery slapped on a winding-up order. David Rowland was exposed to the tune of £6 million. Operationally, the units were so poorly run that even the fundamentals like rent reviews had been missed. Turnover was plummeting, and the potential to make a profit, doubtful.

Rowland had a solution. How would I like to abandon my idea of the commercial properties in Scotland and, instead, take over some of Longman's failed leisure units? My reaction was a flat refusal. I was trying to provide a safe, stable income. This was the antithesis of my plan. I did not want to add more uncertainty to Hibs, and I definitely did not want the task of running a business in which I had no experience.

Rowland was persistent and persuaded me to at least take a look at the leisure properties. On three occasions during the first half of the 1988/89 season, he picked me up from my Swindon office, and we were driven around the units in his chauffeured car. The properties were diverse, both in character and location. A pub in Andover on a lease to the east, a leisure park in Devon to the west. There were several freehold village pubs and some leased city-centre properties, hotels, clubs and restaurants. All of these had massive rents. I remained far from certain that they were the right fit for Hibs.

Rowland was a deal-maker. He could buy and sell with the best (or worst) of them. But he was not an operator. That is a different craft altogether. I didn't think he fully understood the time and skill needed to make these businesses successful. I was already running a legal practice in addition to a major football club. To turn these Avon Inns 'assets' around would require a great deal of skilled attention.

But Rowland was insistent. The flotation had been expensive, as had keeping John Collins and signing Goram and Archie. The company needed more income. And his promises to deliver Scottish properties for Hibs remained unfulfilled. Before the flotation, we had owned the club 40-60 in his favour, and while our stakes had been watered down when Hibs became a PLC, Rowland was still the biggest shareholder.

As an initial investment, Hibs bought The Tavern In The Town. This was a massive freehold pub in Exeter. My mum and dad went down to run it until we could find a longer-term solution. As Hibs could not raise all the money required to buy Avon Inns with a second share issue, Rowland created a new company called Fronstar, which would acquire Avon Inns. Hibs would then purchase the majority shareholding in Fronstar, continuing to buy more of its shares as we progressed.

I was responsible for promoting the deal. I went before the press, championing a group that I still harboured doubts about. The guilt I feel for not making my reservations clear is something I will carry for the rest of my life. I acquiesced, and as a board, we recommended the deal. Naturally, our fans were confused as to why an Edinburgh football club was buying businesses in the West of England. Knowing my connection to that part of the country, some supporters thought it a selfish act instigated by me. In the circumstances, that was quite understandable.

Another lengthy process was undertaken to draft a stock exchange document to acquire Avon Inns. It was a sweet deal for Rowland. He was recouping most of the money he had loaned Longman and was still sitting as the biggest shareholder in Hibs. Rowland would get his original stake back many times over. I would not.

Rather than being offered to individual fans, the new shares in Edinburgh Hibernian PLC from this second issue were directed to the institutional shareholders. I thought it might be telling that I was not taking up the offer myself. Surely, if Avon Inns was such a brilliant investment for the club, someone might ask why not? No one ever did. It became clear there was no chance that the institutions already owning a stake in Edinburgh Hibernian PLC would block the purchase.

While I had handled the original flotation, the acquisition of Avon Inns was managed entirely by Rowland. Beyond being able to testify to his powers of persuasion, I have no idea how he convinced the institutions to further invest. Significantly for what was to come, the balance of power among shareholders had shifted decisively from those concerned with the football team's results and the club's wellbeing to those solely invested in the share price and making a return.

As of March 1989, Avon Inns was owned entirely by Edinburgh Hibernian PLC. I am naturally an optimist, and despite my reservations, I resolved to make this work for Hibs. What choice did I have? The fate of the club and Avon Inns were now inextricably linked. But in retrospect, it proved to be a deal too far – not least because it coincided with one of the worst downturns the British property market had seen for years. David Rowland's timing in offloading Avon Inns to us when he did was exceptional.

The core problem was that the pubs were run by people who acted as owners, not managers. My first action was to insist that the managers of all 13 units fax me their takings and outgoings from the previous day. At best, five would comply. During the past 12 months, they had witnessed at least three owners come and go and were simply not going to take further instructions. I could not sack everybody. I visited, encouraged, cajoled, reprimanded and more, but nothing made any difference. I also put in place a list of suppliers, starting with beer sales. I had made friends with the Courage representative, John Skinner, and he agreed to a scheme enabling us to buy at a discount. There were two tied houses to Bass, but the rest needed to order through Courage. For the restaurants and hotels, I dictated which suppliers they could use. Even the linen for the beds was specified to control costs. They were having none of it. I felt like a football manager who has lost the fabled dressing room from day one.

The man managing our best performing pub had been in post for a decade. He insisted on buying produce from the local supplier, at twice the price, and going to the wholesale shop for his spirits. The previous owner had allowed him to run functions where he did not have to declare his turnover and was allowed to keep all the profits generated. This, he assured me, had been agreed on a handshake. When I explained all revenue belonged to the company, he was very offended. After three warnings, I had no choice but to dismiss him. I thought it would make a statement. No one took heed.

More than a hundred miles away in Bideford, Devon, was Lenwood Country Club. It was the most challenging unit to run, and again, I turned to my parents for help. The property was a beautiful manor house, with a sweeping staircase and a Wren roof window. The problem was that within the grounds, there were 23 chalets, let on long leases. All the occupants had the right to use the manor house, contributing only a basic ground rent. We bore the cost of maintaining it. The indoor swimming pool – I was regularly informed – needed a new roof. Also, "could the squash courts be improved please?"

The leaseholders had long ignored the regulations prohibiting them from residing in the properties for more than 10 months of the year. It turned out that one chalet was being used to run a taxi firm, complete with a radio mast in the garden. A chiropractor and numerous other businesses were working out of the others. The council had finally had enough of this and were threatening to close us down. I could have had a full-time job serving notices but dedicating my time to the task, or employing a solicitor, was not commercially viable.

Another of the Avon Inn units was the Christopher Hotel in Bath. It was a beautiful building where weekend guests could lie in bed and listen to the Abbey choir practising. They sang like angels. Here the difficulty was that we occupied this property on a lease, and our landlords were Bass Charrington. It was a tied house, meaning we had to buy beer and spirits directly from Bass no matter what they charged us.

During Martin Longman's ownership, there had been a rent review. Bass had asked for a highly inflated rent. Longman had failed to do his sums – it was an impossible amount to sustain. Compounding this cock-up, he'd also missed the deadline for renegotiating a lower rent. We were locked into a sinking ship. Later, I discovered this same disaster had been repeated at our second hotel. There too, we were committed to paying rent way above the market value.

Then there were the two restaurants. Popjoys was five-star, high-end and highly-priced. It was formerly a detached house, sitting next to a theatre in Bath. The other was in Bradford-on-Avon. While both establishments bought from the same suppliers, a fillet steak would cost you twice as much at Popjoys as it would in Bradford-on-Avon. On a fact-finding trip, head office discovered a Bradford-on-Avon credit card machine in Popjoys. In an admittedly brilliant swindle, at our expense, colluding staff at the two establishments were putting Popjoys business through a Bradford-on-Avon credit card machine. If a customer bought a £20 fillet steak in Popjoys using a credit card, it would appear as if two £10 steaks had been sold in Bradford-on-Avon. The next time someone paid for a steak in cash in Bradford-on-Avon, the conspirators were then free to pocket the money. Rowland was not interested when I reported these problems to him. He'd extricated himself from the Avon Inns nightmare by dumping it on Hibs. The headache was now mine alone to bear.

When it came to Avon Inns, even the names of the outlets seemed to be cursed. Sainsbury Brothers was a long-established and thriving wholesale wine shop set back from the road on the A4 into Bath. The real jewels of this business were not kept in the front shop but lay instead behind a door in the back office, which like Narnia, led somewhere magical. Kept under lock and key, Sainsbury Brothers housed a collection of the finest wines I'd seen anywhere. Some bottles dated back all the way to 1905. There were three basements, one on top of the other, connected by a rickety staircase. The stock got better and better as you descended through the floors. While I am no sommelier, I knew enough to recognise the riches in the Sainsbury Brothers' cellar. Thankfully, Martin Longman's creditors did not. They agreed to an average price per bottle based on some of the cheaper stuff.

Bafflingly, Sainsbury Brothers did not supply any of the pubs, bars or restaurants that comprised Avon Inns. As usual, when I attempted to instigate any change, I was met with stubborn resistance and hostility. Old-time managers argued that they could get supplies cheaper elsewhere. They could not comprehend that the profit of Sainsbury Brothers belonged to the Avon Inns Group to which they belonged. Put simply, there was no possibility of a cheaper supplier. Every single day, two Sainsbury Brothers' vans would rush past their sister Avon Inns units to stock our competitors. It was utter madness. I like to think of myself as someone who can convince and motivate other people. But at Avon Inns, I became increasingly dictatorial and unhappy. Eventually, all units within the district of Bath complied with my insistence that they use Sainsbury Brothers. It was a pyrrhic victory. I was exhausted.

Upmarket Popjoys had a ridiculously extensive wine list, carrying obscure labels they had no chance of selling. We revamped it and brought in some of the Sainsbury Brothers' 'special' collection. The best was a vintage Chateau Latour, which we put on the restaurant's list at an eye-watering £100 per bottle. For once, our timing was perfect. The theatre next to Popjoys was on the top national circuit where plays would debut before going to the West

End. Such was the calibre of productions, Dustin Hoffman had signed on for an upcoming season. The charming Mr Hoffman used Popjoys frequently, often enjoying a late supper. He worked his way through my champion wine. When his play's run came to an end, there were only two bottles left.

The theatre brought in many other A-listers, and I had an idea to make some of them Hibs ambassadors. My first choice was Paul Eddington, the star of *Yes, Prime Minister*, who I got to know well. I was unaware, however, that he was seriously ill. Just as we were arranging for him to come north for a game at Easter Road, he sadly passed away.

Although Sainsbury Brothers was going well, it needed expert management, which I could not provide. When a potential purchaser contacted me with an offer for the business, I immediately decided to sell. I did all the conveyancing for the company, which was complex and took a long time to reach the point where we could exchange contracts. Just as we were going to sign, I received a letter from the solicitors acting for the supermarket chain of the same name.

The legal firm was a well-known city practice with expertise in intellectual property matters. They demanded that we cease trading using the name 'Sainsbury', claiming we were passing off our service as if it was the supermarket's business. If we did not desist immediately, they threatened to apply to the High Court for an injunction. To save the sale, I had to drop the price and exclude the name. Avon bloody Inns had struck again. This was at least a fight I thought I could win. Taking a robust approach, I argued that as we had been established at the start of the century, long before the supermarket chain had started selling alcohol, the name "Sainsbury Brother Wines" belonged to us. Eventually, I was able to negotiate a settlement in our favour, which exceeded the reduction we'd been forced to offer to push through the sale. This was a rare triumph for Avon Inns. On reflection, perhaps it was the only one.

*

Close by to Sainsbury Brothers, Avon Inns owned a nightclub. We refurbished the venue and installed one of the first-ever laser light shows in the West Country. On the opening night, Fish from the band Marillion was our special guest. He was a great Hibs man and only too happy to help us relaunch the venue. Here finally was one tenuous way we could bring Hibs and Avon Inns together. Very occasionally, Hibs fans would come into the pubs. I made sure there was a Hibs scarf behind the bar and a club crest. They might not have liked their assets, but they did own them.

It would have been so much easier to run this business if it had been in Scotland. Our fans would have flocked to Hibs units in Edinburgh and beyond, ensuring commercial success. For example in Edinburgh, I was happy to recommend the Dean Hotel on the Queensferry Road. The hotel was basic but, being owned by fanatical Hibees, it always offered our fans a warm welcome. Guests could count on returning to a massive party in the Dean's bar after a Hibs win.

Over time, the Dean Hotel formed a branch of the Hibs Supporters' Club, and the Dean Hibs became very proactive in raising money for the youth of Leith. On one occasion, to raise funds they came up with the idea of challenging a Hibs All-Stars team to a charity match. Jim and I were delighted when, out of the blue, Peter Cormack tapped us up to play. I can only think he must have been struggling to make up the numbers.

The game took place at Edinburgh City's ground and was very well supported. It was surreal for me to be getting changed next to legends I'd worshipped as a schoolboy like Pat Stanton and Alex Cropley. They played me up front and did everything they could to get the chairman a goal. Towards the end of the game, a middle-aged-but-still-fit Alex Cropley indicated a place in the six-yard box where he wanted me to run. He then cut inside, beating two players, before rolling a perfectly weighted pass precisely on the spot to which he'd pointed. I found myself unmarked with an open goal at my mercy. I swung my boot. The connection I made was poor, a real scuffer, but thankfully the ball began to trickle towards the goal. Agonisingly, it hit the post. I prepared to turn away, head in hands. But then a cheer went up from the Hibs legends, and I realised the ball had rebounded just across the goal-line. It may not have been the 30-yard screamer I'd always dreamed about scoring in the green jersey, but, as I've told anyone who'll listen ever since, they all count.

I was still looking for ways to try and link Avon Inns in the West Country to Hibernian, or at least to football. With five freehold pubs centred around the market town of Chippenham, I decided to sponsor the local non-league side Chippenham Town. My plan was to informally twin the clubs and promote travel between the two. The idea was well-received. In truth it was not going to cost much because all the Wiltshire club wanted was to have a new strip. And our kit manufacturer, Adidas, were happy to oblige. Avon Inns now adorned the front of the Chippenham Town shirt, and the Hibs team photograph took pride of place in the clubhouse bar.

Around this time, my friend Paul Hatch, who worked at my London office, started a football club called London Hibs. Again, I sourced a kit, and they took to the field each week in the famous green and white. Any Hibees who moved from Scotland to London and could play a bit found a home from home turning out for the Sunday team. As it turned out, London Hibs became a quality side that kept going for many years after my time at Easter Road ended.

*

David Rowland wasn't the first money man to cast a sharp gaze towards football in the 1980s. At the start of the decade, the seemingly unstoppable business titan, Robert Maxwell, had marauded his way through the English First Division. Maxwell was dubbed 'the Bouncing Czech' by the press, a play on his place of birth and colourful financial past. As well as owning Oxford United and Derby County, and having stakes in Reading and Manchester United, he'd agreed to buy Watford from Elton John before the authorities stepped in.

Like David Rowland, Maxwell enjoyed spending much of his time on a vast superyacht. He would float around the ports of the Cote d'Azur while running his business empire remotely by telephone and fax machine. Maxwell's yacht was called 'Lady Ghislaine', named after his now-infamous daughter. Rowland was impressed with Maxwell, and the pair became friendly. When Rowland acquired his own vessel, he followed Maxwell's example by naming it after his own daughter, Venetia. Whenever I had met the real Venetia, she struck me as a gentle, unassuming young woman. The yacht was the opposite.

One afternoon, on the harbour at Antibes, Rowland was kicking a ball about with his young son, Jonathan. Robert Maxwell was passing on foot and joyfully joined the game. Unfortunately, almost with his first kick, he twisted his ankle and was in severe pain. Maxwell, for better or worse, had a seismic influence on English football in the 1980s. But I can reliably report that his claims to have been a flying left-winger in his youth were, like so many of his other stories, fantastical Captain Bob couldn't kick a ball for toffee.

In examining David Rowland's involvement and intentions with Hibs, it is instructive to look at the man today. This will provide context as I tell the rest of my story. Rowland always said his aim was to assist me in building Hibs as a family business for life. Maybe I am naive, but I believed this to be genuine, at least at first. However, when the opportunity to rid himself of his multi-million-pound Avon Inns woes arose, I felt he tossed the grenade to me and Hibs without a second thought.

Rowland later became the owner of the private Banque Havilland based in Luxembourg. He has been a financial adviser and close friend to Prince Andrew and was afforded a front-row seat at the wedding of Andrew's youngest daughter, Princess Eugenie. In 2005, the Prince unveiled a life-size bronze statue of Rowland on the grounds of Rowland's grand estate on Guernsey. His neighbour is the island's governor. The sculptor depicted Rowland puffing a massive cigar, Churchillian style. It wouldn't have been Rowland without it.

Having donated over £4 million to the Conservative Party, in 2010, Rowland was offered the position of party treasurer by then-Prime Minister David Cameron. He accepted the post, but then stepped aside in short order as his tax status and dealings at Hibs came under scrutiny.

In 2018, Luxembourg's financial regulator accused Banque Havilland of flouting Luxembourg's laws designed to prevent money laundering and terrorism financing. It described serious breaches of internal governance, inadequate monitoring of client relationships, and an insufficiently critical mindset among its compliance officers. The bank was later fined €4 million. In 2024, the European Central Bank announced the withdrawal of Banque Havilland's licence.

When it came to football, Rowland and Maxwell both made the same error. For all I know, their thoughts may well have influenced each other. While sharing my view that the game was about to become big business, they failed to understand that you can never truly own a football club. Teams belong to the community and form part of the very DNA of their village, town or city. An inability to appreciate this led both men to believe that deals merging clubs made great 'business sense'. They gave scant consideration to the pain such proposals caused tens of thousands of people.

TEN

THE HAMPDEN DOOR

THE ONLY JOB I would have wanted more at Hibs than being chairman was Jim Gray's. As managing director, he oversaw the club's day-to-day affairs from a ground-floor office located between the changing rooms at Easter Road. I, on the other hand, was always on that bloody shuttle from London to Edinburgh. He did a far better job than I would have done anyway; had I been working at the club full-time, I wouldn't have built the same rapport I enjoyed with the players and staff.

I have always believed that you are only as good as the people around you, which means I've never had any difficulty delegating. In Wiltshire, my secretaries, Lynda and Maureen, were fiercely loyal and extremely capable. In London, Paul and Jane Keeble were two lawyers I held in the highest regard and were people I had known since I was 21. My father was my trouble-shooter at Avon Inns, and I realise now, more than I did at the time, how he tried to protect me from the worst of the stress that came with that nightmare.

But it was Jim Gray who shared my dream for Hibernian and who worked tirelessly to achieve our goals. We rarely fell out and he always consulted me if he thought an idea or a problem required my input. Some of my best ideas may well have been Jim's. We would speak at least twice a day at length, and after all these years, it's impossible to say where a conversation was started and by whom. Our relationship was symbiotic.

Through it all, I also had my own private clients to service. I represented my dear friend, Lesley Manville, during her divorce from Gary Oldman. I advised the man who would become king of Saudi Arabia. And I still took on a bit of legal aid work for those in difficulties but with no resources.

I travelled to Saudi Arabia and will never forget an all-male, late evening picnic in the desert. That night, the company included the head of the Saudi Air Force and a royal prince. We had no booze, of course, but as we ate lamb and smoked the essence of rose water from a shisha pipe, the stars in the sky intoxicated better than anything you'll find in a bottle.

I was invited onto the Prince's Trust. Young businessmen and women met in London about once a month and offered advice and opportunities to the next generation. We also helped to fund their own ideas in a precursor of the *Dragons' Den*. On one occasion, we were to meet at Claridge's Hotel in Mayfair. In my youth, I remembered Claridge's making headlines for refusing The Beatles rooms. This was at the height of the band's fame. The hotel is as much a fixture on the English establishment's circuit as the Boat Race or Chelsea Flower Show. As always, at these sort of events, there was a lavish lunch to enjoy.

After the speeches, I went into a very posh toilet to wash my hands. On my previous visit, there had been an attendant giving out hot towels and cologne. But, on this occasion, the attendant had been stood down. Instead, in his place was one of our landed gentry, hoovering up a line of cocaine from the marble sinks. I quickly left, disappointed if not shocked by what I had seen. I recount this to try to impress upon you what business was really like in Thatcher's Britain. At the supposed highest echelons of our society, there was gratuitous excess and dubious morality. For entirely different reasons, my commitments with Hibs and Avon Inns foremost among them, I dropped out of the Prince's Trust. I later learned many of those held up as examples to the young people had fallen far from the light.

Around this time, a Fulham businessman who used my legal practice introduced me to his accountant, Les Marston, who subsequently became my client. Les was a Scottish chartered accountant, living in a grand house in Southampton with an indoor swimming pool. He had come up with an idea to form leasing companies to let out equipment, funded by his clients, who could expect a massive return. He had no shortage of people ready to invest, and it superficially looked a successful venture.

Later, he started to use his scheme to syndicate the purchase of other assets, such as a massive garden centre. Unbridled capitalism was racing ahead, and the law was struggling to keep pace. Les's problem was that the scale and nature of his burgeoning activities really required him to have a banking licence – which he did not have. The scheme's complexity was beyond the comprehension of the regular police force; instead, it fell to the recently formed Serious Fraud Office to establish the merits of a complaint made against Les. The SFO (as they became known) were fundamentally different to other law agencies. They are expected to seek out grave financial wrongdoing; by contrast, the police investigate and solve the crimes reported to them.

The SFO also had a statutory entitlement to end the right of silence. Refusing to answer their questions was a separate offence, punishable with a maximum of six months' imprisonment. This concept was alien to a young solicitor, who had been trained to keep his clients' business absolutely private. There was a distinct conflict of obligations.

One day, a notice from the SFO arrived at my office. It detailed that Les Marston and his leasing companies were under investigation. In the next paragraph were the names of everyone the SFO wanted to interview as they gathered information against Les. There, on this list, was my name.

Disconcertingly the invitation to attend an interview came with a stark recommendation: I should bring my solicitor with me. My first reaction was to call Les to ask him what was going on. He dismissed the whole affair as an attempt by his business rivals to gain a commercial advantage by nobbling him.

I took the advice on the notice and asked a solicitor friend to accompany me. This was a mistake as the interviewer, a barrister, obviously thought I had something to hide. My concern had been not to breach client-solicitor confidentiality. I have never understood why people are advised to attend interviews with a solicitor if doing so is then considered a sign of guilt. I asked Jane Keeble what she thought. She spoke to her dad, Sir Curtis, on my behalf. His advice was that I should comply, but to keep good notes of what I was being asked. It all seemed routine and nothing I needed to be unduly concerned about. Little did I realise I was becoming entangled in a horror that would have profound significance for this, my Hibs story.

*

The first half of the season had seen us on target to qualify for Europe. I also felt we could win the Scottish Cup. Archie had scored 11 goals, but there was still a feeling among the fans that we needed another forward to share the load. In midfield, Pat McGinlay – a young player cast aside by Blackpool – was getting his chance in our first-team squad and showing great promise. Our first game of the new year saw our third meeting of the season with Hearts. We won 1-0 at Easter Road, Eddie May scoring a fine goal, which meant we were unbeaten six in a row against our local rivals.

In the early months of 1989, we were drawn at home for the first three rounds of the Scottish Cup. Progressing with narrow wins, we set up a semi-final against the mighty Celtic. The Bhoys had romped to the league and cup double in the previous campaign, finishing 10 points clear of Hearts and 12 above Rangers. As we prepared to face them at Hampden Park, the thought that Celtic would fail to win the title for the next nine seasons would have seemed absurd.

Everyone in Scottish football knew that Hibs had not won the Scottish Cup since 1902 and delighted in reminding us of all the distant historical events that had occurred since then. "Even the *Titanic* sank more recently." But having laid the Hearts hoodoo firmly to rest, I felt a sense of destiny as we progressed through each round. I was determined to give fate a helping hand.

In the week before the semi-final, we lodged at a top hotel while training at the Scottish FA's training centre at Largs in Ayrshire. I could sense the confidence beginning to surge through the boys as the Sunday of the game approached. The atmosphere on the team bus to Hampden, however, was subdued. Twenty-four hours earlier, Nottingham Forest had played Liverpool in the English FA Cup semi-final. The horrific pictures of the Hillsborough disaster that ultimately cost 97 people their lives were fresh in our minds. There was to be a minute's silence before our match. Both teams were to wear black armbands as a sign of respect to those who had died. This was the old Hampden Park with the grand entrance hall and huge, sweeping, open terraces. Looking at the tens of thousands of happy fans clad in green and white, it was impossible to comprehend how in South Yorkshire an occasion like this had resulted in such horror.

I had invited some Celtic-supporting Irish business associates to be my guests at the game, and I prepared to be suitably

Right: David Rowland puffing on one of his trademark cigars. *Eyevine*

Below: Succession: Kenny Waugh and I are all smiles after finally completing the protracted negotiations that saw me become Hibs chairman. *Newsprints*

The New Board – me, Sheila Rowland and Jim Gray in 1987. Sheila helped me buy the club. Much more importantly, three years later, she helped save it. *Mirrorpix*

Welcoming four of the 'Famous Five' back to Easter Road. *Newsprints*

Wallace Mercer and I force a smile for the camera. In truth we were very different people and chairmen. *Mirrorpix*

Yes, Prime Minister – Wallace Mercer and Jim Gray meet the 'Iron Lady'. *Alamy*

Musician Colin Chisholm may be a Jambo but he gave Hibs a fantastic
anthem and our very own greyhound Cabbage and Ribs. *Newsprints*

Paul Kane giving it everything in the derby. During my time at Hibs we ended a decade of hurt
by beating Hearts home and away. Edinburgh has two great teams with their own proud traditions.
The idea of 'Edinburgh United' was anathema to me and the supporters of both clubs. *Getty Images*

There's no place like home. Jim Gray welcomes Mickey Weir back to Easter Road with some champagne donated by a fan. *Newsprints*

John Collins and The Proclaimers model our new kit. *Mirrorpix*

Scotland's number 1. Andy Goran may have caused me more than th odd headache but he was a brillian goalkeeper with an enormou heart. *Getty Images*

Did you ever hear about the time Hibs signed a top striker from Barcelona? I'm positively glowing here after completing one of the greatest transfer coups in Scottish football history that brought Steve Archibald to Easter Road. *Getty Images*

Police rush on to the Easter Road pitch to help those fans affected by the CS Gas canister thrown by an idotic Celtic supporter. It was one of the most frightening moments of my life. *Newsprints*

Brave New World: Floating Hibs on the stock market proved to be a game changer but not in the way I had planned. *Mirrorpix*

'We're all going on a European Tour' – Happy Hibees in
Belgium ahead of our UEFA Cup tie with Royal Liege. *Newsprints*

Alex Miller tries to rouse the boys for extra-time against
Liege but sadly our European adventure ended there. *Newsprints*

Disappointingly, the Tennents' Sixes was the only silverware we
won during my tenure. I'd hoped for much more. *Getty Images*

'Hands Off Hibs': Fans make their feelings clear at the Easter Road rally to oppose the bid. *Getty Images*

Over My Dead Body: Clutching the defence document that ultimately saw off Wallace Mercer and his toxic bid for Hibernian. *Newsprints*

Sir Tom Farmer taking in the action at Easter Road. *Getty Images*

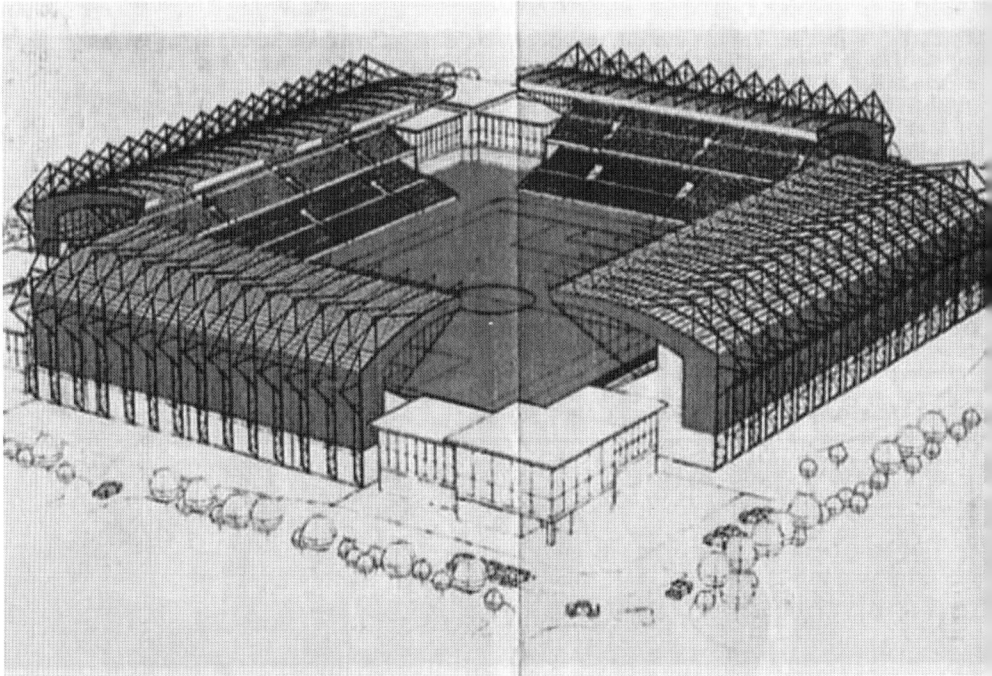

The stadium that never was. A design of the proposed New Easter Road at Straiton. *Edinburgh Evening News*

On set in my new life as an actor for the BBC sketch show *Famalam*

humble in victory. Sadly, the match did not work out that way. Within the opening 30 minutes, Celtic were three-nil ahead. At half-time, attempting to collect my thoughts and hide my disappointment, I wandered out to the front of the stadium where our coach was parked. After five minutes of deep breathing, I felt sufficiently composed to return and made my way back to the entrance. "Have you got a ticket please, Mr Duff?" The request came from an old soldier guarding the door and sporting enough silverware on his chest to melt down and make a new Scottish Cup if required.

I explained that I had left my ticket upstairs. As he clearly knew who I was – given that he had addressed me by name, not to mention that I was wearing my official club blazer and tie – I asked would he please forgive my absent-mindedness? "Sorry, Mr Duff, if you don't have your ticket, you cannot come in." Next, I tried to reason with him. "As we are three-nil down, I'm hardly likely to be a gatecrasher, am I?" But still, he refused me entry. At this point, I saw red and regrettably unleashed a barrage of industrial language. Had it not been for dear Ernie Walker spotting me and politely instructing the old boy to let me in, I probably would have spent the second half in the Hampden car park. Our performance after the interval was better. Archie scored a goal to give us a glimmer of hope, but Celtic then shut up shop. Our cup dream was over for another year. The game taught me to manage my expectations. We still had a long way to go to match the great Hibs teams of the past.

Three days after our Hampden disappointment, the team edged to a 1-0 victory in the league against St Mirren. Archie was again on the scoresheet. He followed this up with a brace against Hamilton Academical in a 3-0 victory. This sealed fifth place in the league and secured us a UEFA Cup spot at the expense of Hearts. It was the first time we had finished above them in the table for six seasons. We were now without question the best team in Edinburgh.

*

At the end of the 1988/89 campaign, Jim and I were at Selhurst Park for the second leg of the English Second Division play-off semi-final between Crystal Palace and Swindon Town. Swindon had won the first leg 1-0 and, as I knew so many people at the club, I was desperate for them to win. It was not to be.

The play-offs represent one final chance for football people to gather before the long summer break. The Selhurst Park boardroom was full of those squeezing the last drops of enjoyment from the season. Sitting on his own in the corner of the room was Kenny Dalglish. Kenny, as always, was happy not being the centre of attention. Liverpool had beaten Everton in an all-Merseyside FA Cup final four days earlier. Jim and I went over to chat with him. I congratulated Liverpool on winning the FA Cup and offered my condolences for what had happened at Hillsborough.

It was hard to know what to say to a man who had been through such trauma. He was now carrying the entire weight of a grieving city on his shoulders. Kenny had also witnessed first-hand the carnage of Heysel in 1985 and the Ibrox disaster in 1971. The loss of life on those two occasions had not been heeded. Britain's crumbling old stadiums combined with the authorities' perception that football fans were a threat to law and order had proven lethal that day in Sheffield. In the aftermath of Hillsborough, it was clear that long-overdue change to the national game had to come. The terraces would be torn down and replaced with family-friendly, all-seater grounds.

In Scotland, only a few clubs like Aberdeen and St Johnstone had all-seater stadiums. St Johnstone had moved to the outskirts of Perth, helped by one of Edinburgh's invisible elite. Architect and property developer Grant Butchart had negotiated for Asda to build a superstore on their old Muirton Park ground. In exchange, the Saints would receive a fully-paid-for, purpose-built new stadium on the Perth ring road.

Hillsborough triggered many similar moves. Clubs found they could relocate from landlocked city-centre sites to new stadiums on the edge of town, with modern conveniences for fans and extensive parking. The value of the land occupied by clubs in city centres meant not only could new grounds be funded, but there were also large profits to be made. New stadiums were built with inexpensive, prefabricated materials. Supermarkets would gladly fund building them to unlock desirable acreage for their stores. Football clubs were happy to obtain modern grounds at little or no expense.

The question for our board was, should Hibs move from Easter Road? As we shall see later, the various property developers who began circling Hibernian – and more specifically the club's prime Edinburgh land – understood the price of everything but the value of nothing.

As well as throwing up questions about our stadium, the close season of 1989 also saw the club's management bowled a googly by one of our players. There is only one man who has played both football and first-class international cricket for Scotland.

His name was Andy Goram. That summer, Andy, a keen cricketer since his youth, was selected to play for Scotland's cricket team against the touring Australians. When he asked Alex Miller for permission to take part, his request was summarily dismissed. For Andy, it was a once-in-a-lifetime opportunity. For us, it was a potential nightmare. A stray ball from an Australian bat could endanger the handsome living he was making from football and rob us of our keeper. As a club, we needed to protect one of our prized assets. Andy being Andy, he decided to play anyway. The goalie was fined the maximum sum allowed. "Chairman," he said afterwards, "it was worth every penny."

All fines collected from players over the season were given to the Hibs Supporters' Association or used to buy Christmas presents for underprivileged local children. The previous Christmas, Andy effectively played Santa as he had been the only player fined.

Andy's sporting prowess extended beyond football and cricket. Our sponsors, Frank and Robert Graham, owned a snooker hall, very close to Easter Road across Leith Walk. It was popular with players and fans alike. Goram, again in keeping with his keen eye and appreciation of angles, was a talented player. On a celebrity night, he challenged future snooker world champion, John Parrott, to a match. Parrott was doing a promotion in Edinburgh but took time out to accept Andy's invitation. Remarkably, over three frames Andy beat him two to one.

Knowing Andy as I did, I think he will have been tickled by the chant that followed his mild schizophrenia being made public. "There's only two Andy Gorams."

Shortly after Goram's adventure with the Aussies, in August 1989, I received a phone call from Jim Kean at the *Daily Record*: "Do you know who Michael Knighton is?" I didn't, but I promised I would ring around my contacts to see what they knew. My interest was piqued. Knighton, explained Kean, had just bought Manchester United. Martin Ferguson, my usual source for Old Trafford gossip, was in the dark about Knighton. So too, he said, was his brother.

On the opening Saturday of the new 1989/90 season, Knighton announced himself to Alex Ferguson and the rest of the world. Borrowing a strip from the Old Trafford home dressing room, he took to the pitch to show off his ball skills ahead of United's fixture with reigning league champions Arsenal. Fergie and his players were astonished. I have absolutely no doubt Knighton would have picked himself to play in the game if he'd thought he could get away with it.

I've never been shy, so I decided to call Martin Edwards, whom I had not met before, believing he would speak to me chairman to chairman. I was right. Edwards seemed to have only very sketchy information about Knighton. He had made precious few background checks on the prospective buyer of the club he had inherited from his father. For reasons I would discover later, Knighton's bid came at a fortuitous time. Martin Edwards wanted out of the public eye. His decision to sell United had been made almost on a whim. He believed Knighton had a substantial backer, but he hadn't thought it necessary to ask who. Our conversation concluded with Martin inviting me down to Old Trafford for a game in the new season. Over the next year, we became friends. Knighton, however, for now, remained a very high-profile enigma.

Our pre-season filled me with hope. Keith Houchen, signed from Coventry for £325,000 in March of the previous campaign, looked incredibly sharp in our warm-up matches. And with the addition of Brian Hamilton, we felt the squad was finally ready to mount a serious challenge for silverware. Notwithstanding my troubles in the West Country and dealings with the Serious Fraud Office, I went into the 1989/90 season full of belief. A year would prove to be a long time in football.

ELEVEN

WE'RE ALL GOING ON A EUROPEAN TOUR

FEW PEOPLE BEYOND Easter Road know that Hibs were the first British club to play in the European Cup. European football has been an integral part of Hibernian's identity ever since. In 1955 Hibs had finished fifth in the league but were invited to participate in the newly conceived competition to crown the continent's top team; they reached the semi-final. This invite was due to another Leith-born chairman, Harry Swan, whose achievements outstripped mine by a country mile.

In addition to leading Hibernian during the club's glorious 'Famous Five' era, Swan became president of the Scottish Football Association in 1952. While the insular English FA banned First Division champions Chelsea from taking part in the European Cup and other Scottish clubs opted out believing the cost of travelling overseas would eclipse any revenue generated by the matches, Swan proved to be a visionary. His decision to enter Hibs into a tournament including the likes of AC Milan, Real Madrid and Sporting Clube de Portugal was instrumental in winning British hearts and minds to the idea of a Europe-wide club competition.

It was only once I departed Hibernian that I researched Swan, but his ambition for the club could have been sentiments uttered from my own mouth: "I want to make Hibernian one of the finest teams in the land." Also, "I would like to think that, at Hibernian, we had always been an outward-looking club."

Qualification for Europe after an 11-year absence had seen us reach a critical milestone in my plan for Hibs. Even the increasingly bleak outlook for Avon Inns couldn't dampen my excitement at the prospect of Ajax, Atletico Madrid, Juventus, Napoli or Paris Saint-Germain running out at Easter Road. To try and turn Avon Inns around, I had suggested to David Rowland that I work closely with Jeremy James, his right-hand man. Jeremy, who Rowland appointed to the club's board, had grown fond of Hibs. I hoped a trip to see the second leg of the 1989 UEFA Cup final between Stuttgart and Napoli would whet his appetite further. On the pitch, the sublime Diego Maradona secured an aggregate victory for Napoli. Off the pitch, as we spoke about Avon Inns, it became abundantly clear Jeremy had no positive advice to offer. Avon Inns needed capital. But having clawed back the money he'd lost, David Rowland was most definitely out. It would remain my burden alone.

I tried to shield my growing concern from Jim and Alex as we travelled to Geneva at the start of the new season for the UEFA Cup draw. Each club is represented by a similar delegation of manager, chief exec and chairman. After the draw, you'd meet with your counterparts from the opposition to arrange logistics for the tie. The executives dealt with hotels, travel, hospitality and, most importantly, player and fan safety. The managers discussed training facilities, access to the home ground and generally had a good gossip. Or, at least, that's how it's meant to work. Teams would have to find each other by shouting their opponent's name. The noise was deafening. To an observer, it must have sounded like the Tower of Babel.

The European Cup was drawn first. Then came the Cup Winners' Cup. Before finally, a shattered master of ceremonies

turned to the UEFA Cup. "Hibernian will play . . . Videoton."
It was a name I had a distant memory of hearing before, but I
had no idea which country they were from. Alex confirmed our
opponents were Hungarian and had knocked out Manchester
United en route to losing to Real Madrid in the 1985 UEFA
Cup final. We would not be the favourites.

Before we could get our heads around the prospect of a
trip to Communist Eastern Europe, our first task was to
navigate the perimeter of the room, seeking out the Videoton
delegation. We passed AC Milan and Barcelona. There must
have been eight officials each from those two titanic clubs. After
circumnavigating the entire room, we concluded that Videoton
had simply not turned up for the draw. What could we do? We
found Honved from Budapest. "Have you seen Videoton?" The
reply in Hungarian offered us little help.

Eventually, we went up to the high podium, where an official
confirmed that Videoton had signed in. They were out there
somewhere. So, we looked again. Still no joy. "Let's go to the bar,"
I suggested. A narrow flight of stairs led us to a quiet cocktail bar
where we ordered a drink and prepared to resume the search.

There, in the corner, was Ottó Brávácz, president of Videoton,
with his coach and sidekicks. 'Egeszsegedre' was the first
Hungarian word I learned. It means bottoms up. We were the
only teams drawn that made their arrangements at the bar.
Hungary and Scotland were going to be a potent combination.
Ottó did not speak English, nor I Hungarian, and we conducted
our talks in pidgin German, sign language and laughter.

We were drawn at home in the first leg and resolved that we
would be the best possible host. I offered the Dragonara Hotel,
a very comfortable four-star on the edge of the New Town.
Ottó wanted a team bus. No problem. He asked whether he
would need a car, and I promised him one and a driver to take
him wherever he wanted. Videoton would be in Edinburgh for

two nights. Most teams spend only one night away and tend to fly home directly after the match. I always thought that a day acclimatising was sensible and a night off afterwards essential. Ottó agreed.

I learned that Videoton were based in Szekesfehervar, a small city about 40 miles south of Budapest. The city was once the Hungarian capital, back when the country was ruled by kings and emperors. Videoton was like a smaller version of PSV Eindhoven, in that it had started out as a works team. The factory of the same name made televisions. The difference was that most able men in the city still worked for Videoton.

We would need to carefully manage the away leg. Such was the thirst for European football among our fans, we were able to sell our full allocation of 2,000 for a trip that would take us inside supposed Cold War 'enemy' lines. Jane Keeble in my London office had some sage advice from her family, who were experienced travellers in Eastern Europe. "Leave nothing to chance. Book everything well in advance, right down to the meals the players will eat at the hotel."

Jane's father, Sir Curtis, chair of the Great Britain-USSR Association, said we would be surprised at how quickly things were unravelling in the Eastern Bloc. He suggested we head out on a fact-finding mission to see for ourselves. We took their advice, and Jim and I did a 'recce' of three nights.

Budapest was a great surprise. There appeared to be little poverty there. The only clues that we were not in the West were the very colourful people selling caviar on the street. That and a queue of about 50 youngsters outside the Adidas shop buying what they thought were the latest fashions. In reality, they were nothing short of retro. The city was stunning, with beautiful architecture and warm people. The river Danube dissected Budapest. To the west was the city's wonderful castle on the hilltop. On the eastside were the palatial administration buildings of the Austro-Hungarian Empire. The Danube had followed the fault line, splitting two very different geographical areas as well as the city. This fault produced heavenly sulphur spas with hot water coming straight out of the ground.

I would later learn that Hungary never experienced the poverty of some of its neighbours. The Danube flood basin produced rich, agricultural soil in which to grow plentiful crops. I remember being told how, at the end of the Cold War, Soviet troops in Hungary were confined to barracks until they withdrew. The authorities did not want the soldiers to see that the Hungarians had a surplus of food when in Moscow, families were forced to queue in the stark streets for essentials.

When we arrived at Szekesfehervar, it was not quite so grand as the capital had been. In fact, there was only one half-decent hotel. We would need that for the team and the official party. The majority of the fans would have to stay in Budapest and travel down for the match. In our modern world of global communication, it may come as a shock to the reader that the whole of Szekesfehervar had only three telephone lines out of the city. To call home, you had to book the line hours in advance. And it was pot luck if you would get a connection.

During our tour out to Videoton's Sostoi Stadium, we were told it had no segregation. There was only one road in and out, which worried me. It was typically Soviet, a dour concrete bowl with a running track around the pitch. Ottó was pleased to see us, although he quickly changed the subject when I asked if we could have a look around the Videoton television factory. The luxury Mercedes Videoton team bus I spotted parked up outside seemed incongruous. Ottó explained that he had acquired the vehicle from a top Italian club. It was part payment of a transfer fee for one of his players.

I loved Hungary and looked forward to coming back with the Hibs team. First, however, we had to play host. I am sure many of the clubs who play in Europe, year in, year out, have executives who would not understand our level of preparation or excitement.

Before the Hungarians arrived in Edinburgh on 10 September, 1989, our start to the season had been mixed. We had beaten Rangers and a good Dundee United side 2-0 at Easter Road, but had lost our two away games to Aberdeen and Hearts, both by a single goal. Some of our fans were beginning to grumble about Alex Miller and his style of play. But that was all put to one side as we waited in anticipation in the Turnhouse lounge as the Soviet Tupolev aeroplane touched down. We welcomed our visitors onto the bus. Hibs were back in the big time.

To celebrate the arrival of our Hungarian guests, we arranged a traditional Scottish dinner for the Videoton party, the referee and his linesmen and the UEFA official. A piper played in the haggis. There were kilts, the full works. The splendid dinner was organised by Lothian Region, and Jimmy Cook gave a great speech. Mine was nowhere near as entertaining, but I hoped it expressed my heartfelt welcome. Throughout all this, the Hibs team, to the best of my knowledge, were tucked up in their beds.

The next morning, Videoton trained at Easter Road. I watched them and was very impressed. They were slick passers and had one or two players who could shoot devastatingly from long range. I mentioned this to Andy Goram at our team meal before the game. "Let them shoot from where they like. Nothing is getting past me, chairman."

The teams were led to the field by two pipers. Videoton were becoming very familiar with Scotland's famous musical instrument. I was so nervous that my memories of the actual match are sparse, but it was a very tight affair. I do clearly remember our ginger-topped defender, Graham Mitchell, scoring the only goal. Graham played a massive 265 games for Hibs. He scored four goals, none more significant than this.

As the Hungarians departed Edinburgh, the tie remained very much in the balance. Our lead was slender, but we had avoided conceding the dreaded away goal. Football moves on quickly, and four days later, St Mirren visited us in the league. Confidence was high. We won 3-1 with Houchen netting twice and John Collins also on the scoresheet.

Our preparations for the return leg in Hungary had been meticulous. In the build-up, Jane asked me if I could deliver an envelope from her father to an embassy official at Budapest Airport. I agreed, wondering why the letter could not be sent via the diplomatic pouch?

One of the most taxing tasks involved in organising the trip had been arranging a charter flight. Such an operation did not come cheap. Jim and I had flown Malev Hungarian Airlines on our reconnaissance mission. The Malev aeroplanes were Soviet and very manoeuvrable. In case of war, the Tupolev range of aircraft could be turned into warplanes by simply refitting the nose. The pilots were trained in the style of Dan Dare, while the interior of the planes resembled an old British Rail carriage, and a web of ropes secured the overhead luggage. Suffice to say, of three or four quotes, Malev were the most competitive by a considerable distance. Our requirement was for 30 seats. Their plane could accommodate 200. We saw a chance to cover the charter cost by offering a package to the fans: flight, hotel and match ticket. The offer sold out immediately. We were going to be well supported.

My own parents, family and friends were all coming. It was going to be an unforgettable experience for everyone involved. I heard some incredible stories afterwards of the fun people had in Budapest. I am sure reading this, there will be a few knowing smiles on the faces of those who were there. Being with the team was a completely different experience. It was all very quiet and intense. We decided the boys should travel to Hungary in Hibs tracksuits, and they were all issued with new ones. You'd be amazed how something seemingly trivial like a new club tracksuit can boost a football team's morale and sense of occasion.

Ahead of the trip, I had been in regular contact with Ottó. I repeatedly checked that the security measures we'd asked for were in place, and questioned him about how they were planning to manage crowd segregation. He just laughed and told me to stop worrying.

These weeks were among my favourite times at Hibs, even with the shadow of Avon Inns looming large. It saddened me that David Rowland did not feel that our return to Europe marked an opportunity to create an enduring legacy. Hibernian should have been something he felt proud of. Sheila, by contrast, was travelling to Budapest as a fan. What had started as a job for her had developed into a passion. In retrospect, I should have used this time as an opportunity to challenge Rowland. I was too young and naive to the way 'the game' is played by people like him. I desperately wanted to believe he would eventually see what he had in Hibs. However, Hungary beckoned, and he was not coming.

The team would travel under a joint sports visa. The authorities in the East were well practised at hosting Western football teams, making this relatively easy to arrange. The rest of us required individual entry clearance. The players were briefed to meet at Easter Road from where they would be bussed to the airport in good time in their new tracksuits. The directors would meet them there in official green club blazers and ties. We were ready.

*

I love those mornings of purpose when I wake up excited at the prospect of the day ahead. I don't think I have ever felt that buzz more than I did on that bright autumnal morning we were scheduled to fly to Hungary. It didn't last long.

When we got to the airport, our charter had not arrived. Enquiries revealed that it had left Budapest but was still nearly two hours away. We decided to hold the team at Easter Road and call them in when our plane was on final approach to Edinburgh.

The airport itself was like a giant Hibs convention. There was green and white everywhere. As well as our official charter, there were a couple of other planes carrying our fans. Some people were flying to Amsterdam and London for connecting flights to Budapest. I was happy to be delayed and soak up the atmosphere. Later, I was told that many more Hibees travelled by road. We felt like a very good-natured invading army.

When, at last, the big jet came lumbering in, it was unlike any plane I had seen before. I immediately suppressed any thoughts about the physics required to keep it airborne. The team arrived looking immaculate. At the desk, Cecil collected all their passports. "Where's your passport, Mickey?" asked Cecil. "It's on the living room sideboard," was wee Mickey Weir's nonchalant reply. Alex made some reference to the lad going forth and multiplying. Apparently, Mickey thought travel behind the Iron Curtain did not require such trifling details as a passport.

Like a scene from a Hollywood thriller, Peter and Mickey were dispatched in a taxi, racing through the streets of Edinburgh to reach the Weir family sideboard. We decided to start boarding the flight hoping against hope our errant winger wouldn't cost us our slot on the runway. Those on the club package boarded through the back door while the team, officials and press went into the front. A little curtain separated the two sections. It really did feel like a massive family holiday. Edinburgh is a small town, Leith is smaller still. Everyone knew everyone, one joyous tribe.

The fans were not going to wait for the stewardesses to bring round the complimentary drinks. Even though it was still before noon and not everyone had found their seat, carry-ons appeared throughout the cabin. When Peter and Mickey finally appeared, they must have wondered if they were on a flight to the Costa del Sol rather than a UEFA Cup tie. There were four stewardesses. Two were very imposing, stern-looking ladies. But despite their stature, they couldn't control the green-and-white horde. Eventually, the captain explained that he could not take off until everyone was seated. This finally did the trick, although many of the fans were up again talking to their pals before the plane reached cruising height.

About 45 minutes into the journey, the two formidable stewardesses started to deliver complimentary drinks from the trolley. The players were on soft drinks, while I allowed myself a solitary glass of red. After all, it was nearly lunchtime.

I was sitting next to an *Evening News* reporter, giving an interview on our trip, when I spotted the tallest stewardess making her way down the aisle handing out refreshments. Suddenly, there came an enormous roar from the back of the cabin. One of the fans had clocked that their 'trolley dolly' was none other than Andy Goram. With the help of two or three teammates, Andy had gone to the front and charmed one of the Malev team to lend him their jacket, apron and bright red lipstick. A mop on his head completed the disguise, and he had served drinks to half the plane before being rumbled. This was Andy Goram at his best, and it prompted a chorus of Hibs songs as we passed through the clouds above Europe.

On arrival, the official party were diverted through a private exit leading straight to a waiting bus. This meant that I could not pass on the letter Jane had asked me to deliver. My years of training in keeping client secrets ensured my curiosity didn't get the better of me. The envelope remained unopened in my jacket pocket.

We were whisked straight to our hotel in the city of Szekesfehervar. The boys were billeted two or three to a room, which suited them fine. Most players, in my experience, prefer the company of teammates rather than being alone when away from home. On our first reconnaissance visit, we had noticed each room contained an old-fashioned fridge brimming with assorted beverages. We asked the hotel staff to remove the alcohol before the players checked in.

The stadium had a capacity of around 15,000, so we had no worries that the players would be overawed. We arranged for the team to do some light training on the pitch to acclimatise to conditions. We had taken two hampers of our own food with us. Hungarian cuisine is delicious, but a change in diet can be performance-wrecking, and Alex wanted to take no chances.

On the eve of the game, the players were shown one last tactical video, before being instructed to get an early night. By contrast, the Hibs board members were treated to a traditional Hungarian reception. Our host and my counterpart, Ottó, was determined to return our hospitality. In fact, it had turned into a competition between us.

A minibus collected our party, and we were driven down a dark road before finally coming to a stop in dense woods where we were told to alight. The driver pointed down an unlit path and I'll admit to being more than a little frightened. I half expected a Soviet sniper to open fire from behind a tree. Eventually, we arrived at a clearing where we were warmly greeted by the Videoton executives. After a sumptuous meal of goulash, and a good portion of Bull's Blood wine and sweet Tokaj, we began to exchange songs.

'Hail, Hail', 'Hibs Heroes' and 'The Hibs Go Marching On' came from our raucous side of a long oak table. The Hungarian songs, by contrast, were sombre and depressing. They were accompanied by two men in traditional folk dress with accordions. It was music for a funeral. Unable to understand the words, I imagined the lyrics were lamenting a lost time long ago. When I asked, Ottó told me they were solemn songs of patriotism, sung with pride. Deep down, I hoped they would have further cause to sing their sad tunes the next evening once the full-time whistle blew.

We then began swapping some football stories. They spoke of the great Hungarian team of the 1950s, which with stars like Puskás, Kocsis and Hidegkuti had come so painfully close to lifting the World Cup in 1954. Liverpool had been the great British team of the 1970s and early 80s, and Ottó was keen to hear tales of the great Bill Shankly. I soon recounted Shankly's famous maxim: "Football is not a matter of life and death. It's much more important than that."

Our Hungarian hosts were enthralled. I explained that I had once attended a dinner where Shanks had been the honoured guest speaker. Rising to his feet, Shankly had looked around the room before saying, "See yous, I went to a wedding last week and took this beautiful young lady up the aisle. I realised that I hardly knew her because I was too busy working all the time. Go home and be with your families." I imagined the remark about his daughter's wedding was far more how Shankly felt than the famous quote. What a man he was.

It may not have been the most important day of my life, but 26 September, 1989, was definitely the best I ever had in football. Ottó wanted to put on another lunch banquet. We were still recovering from the night before and asked politely for something simple at our hotel where our players would take their pre-game nap before the evening kick-off. There, on a veranda, Jim, Alex, Peter and I passed a cold, sunny afternoon enjoying a beer with Ottó, the Videoton coach Gábor Kaszás and his assistant.

Ottó told us the history of his town. He predicted Hungary would soon change in these days of perestroika. As a senior member of the Communist Party, he viewed this with trepidation. Later that night after the game, I would discover why he had declined to show us around the Videoton factory on our first visit. In a drunken moment of indiscretion, Ottó let slip that in addition to televisions, the plant also made components for the USSR's guided missiles. It was a secret only he and a few trusted workers were privy to. It did not fit with the new realpolitik of the time. He may well have been pulling my leg, but there was no doubt that Ottó's world was changing. After Hungary became a democracy, I heard that Ottó came to be viewed with deep suspicion. I hope the rumour I was told that he ended up serving time in prison was false. I have tried to reconnect with him in recent years, but have never managed to reach him.

Our deep pre-match conversation about shifting political tectonic plates was interrupted when two peanuts rebounded off my head. I swivelled, scanning the empty balconies from where I thought they had come. They proved the opening salvo in a barrage of tasty Hungarian snacks that began raining down on us. The accompanying boyish giggle was unmistakable. The perpetrator was none other than our esteemed goalkeeper, Andy Goram.

Throughout the day, the town began to swell with Hibees who had made their way from Budapest. After the players had eaten their carefully prepared pre-game meal, we boarded the bus for the stadium. There were about a hundred fans gathered at the front of the hotel to wave us off. As the coach made its way through the streets, we put on the cassette 'Sunshine on Leith' by The Proclaimers. The volume was cranked up as high as it would go, and as the words seeped into us, we felt like gladiators preparing to enter the Colosseum.

Every road on our short journey to the stadium was packed with Hibs fans. We looked out at them as the music reverberated around the coach. It was a call to arms, a moment that still brings a lump to my throat more than 30 years on. 'Sunshine on Leith' has come to define the club and, in my view, will never be surpassed as the greatest Hibs anthem of them all. Few, however, will know that its origins as the ultimate football song were founded on a coach in faraway Hungary.

As the game kicked off, I was pleased to see Alex had set the team up to play on the front foot. An early away goal would kill the tie. It was a bold move. He proved that night he could send sides out onto the park to attack. After nine minutes, we got our reward as Keith Houchen scored. We sat there doing the maths. Videoton would now need three goals to progress.

Any chance of a Videoton comeback was ended in the 52nd minute. Tamás Petres threw a punch and was dismissed from the field, leaving the struggling hosts down to 10 men. Shortly after, Gareth Evans tapped in a second before John Collins completed the rout with a third.

I had worried during the game about the terrible lack of segregation within the ground. Although our official ticket allocation gave Hibs fans the enclosure under the main stand, there was green and white wherever you looked in the stadium. Thankfully, it all went off peacefully and in good humour. The fans in the main stand would not leave the stadium after the game, determined to enjoy the occasion for as long as possible. Jim and I went onto the pitch, where we conducted them in Hibs songs, including our new anthem from the coach. No doubt the chief put 'Sunshine on Leith' that night.

After the game, the two teams went back to the hotel for a gala reception. The boys tried their best to raise a smile from their subdued Videoton counterparts. We let the players continue their celebrations in the small town centre. They received a heroes' welcome from those fans who were staying on in Hungary.

Ottó disappeared late in the evening, and it wasn't until morning we located him asleep on a park bench. I can only imagine how much he enjoyed Videoton's victories if this was how he took defeat. On the very next bench was one of our players, also well oiled. He shall remain nameless. The whole official party were nursing world-class hangovers on the coach back to Budapest.

There we passed the Liberty Statue, which sits atop Gellert Hill, overlooking the Danube. She holds in her outstretched hands a giant palm leaf of peace. During the night, a Hibs fan had somehow climbed the monument and placed, between her palms, two Hibs scarves tied together. It was a touching sight to behold.

I finally met my man from the embassy at the airport, handing him what was, by now, a very crumpled and dirty envelope. To this day, I do not know what secrets were contained inside. Full of exhausted passengers, the flight home was significantly quieter than the one that brought us to Budapest. It had been the trip of a lifetime.

*

The UEFA and Cup Winners' Cup were far more prestigious in the days of straight knockout football than in the swollen group stage of today's Europa and Conference League. There weren't endless preliminary rounds or seedings; massive clubs could fall at the first hurdle. Every chance was your only chance. The further you progressed, the more you created a profile in Europe. Through the managerial brilliance of Alex Ferguson and Jim McLean, unknown Aberdeen and Dundee United came to be feared citadels on the European footballing map. We flew out to Switzerland for the second-round draw, hoping a big scalp could elevate Hibernian in the same way.

Before leaving, I took a call from an Italian television executive. He wanted to agree on an option for the broadcast rights for our game, in the event of us drawing an Italian club. The maths were relatively straightforward. There were 32 teams in the velvet bag, and three were Italian: Fiorentina, Juventus and Napoli. It was around 10-1 that we would draw one of them. The executive's offer was £5,000. Given the probability, it seemed like money for nothing. Television companies were finally waking up to the value of having live football on their channels. This meant securing rights for matches that might never happen. I chanced my arm. "We'll take £50,000." He laughed and, after some banter, we resolved to meet in Switzerland to continue negotiations.

An hour before the draw was made, I met him and his lawyer. The Italians produced a standard form of contract, both in Italian and English. They had inserted £10,000 as the option fee. This represented a good bonus for Hibs, but I felt we could do better. We eventually settled on £18,000, but still had to formalise the contract.

The draw was about to start, so Jim and Alex left me locked in a room with the television exec and his lawyer. By the time we had all signed on the dotted line, the identity of our next opponents was revealed. Hibernian would play Belgium's Royal Liege. Jim and Alex had already met their delegation and agreed upon preliminary arrangements. I was disappointed to have missed the draw, but the easy money I earned for the club was a decent consolation. I can only speculate what the Italian television viewing figures would have been for Hibs vs Liege.

Our Belgian opponents were far more demanding than Videoton had been about the logistics for their trip to Scotland. Liege declined the hotel we offered. And after much back and forth, we agreed to put them up at the Holiday Inn on Queensferry Road. Although the regional authority was again keen to host them and organise an Edinburgh tour, Liege did not want a grand civic reception. Instead, they confirmed they were going to make their stay in Scotland as brief as possible.

For me, the weeks between the two UEFA Cup rounds were predominantly spent at Avon Inns. I was implementing yet more basic business practices in a desperate attempt to increase turnover. The units were stubbornly refusing to turn a profit, and our debt was growing. Interest rates were at an all-time high.

We urgently needed to start seeing some progress. Our financiers were the Bank of Scotland, and at this time, they still seemed supportive of our endeavours. No doubt Rowland's involvement in Hibs, however distant, and the reputation of our institutional shareholders inspired the bank's confidence.

Our senior contact at the bank was Gavin Masterton, a massive football enthusiast and a man who will play a crucial part later in this story. Masterton was the managing director and treasurer of the Bank of Scotland. He would have been instrumental in the death of Hibs had we let him. In years to come, his designs on football would contribute to his own spectacular downfall.

Rowland began to fixate on the idea of reducing the PLC's debt by selling Hibs' best players. I spent a morning trying to show him that this was the exact opposite of the plan we'd agreed when he invested in the club. The commercial enterprise was supposed to support the club, not be served by it. "Don't buy any more players," he cautioned me. I had by now lost all faith in him. While he was the major shareholder, I remained the chairman with the board behind me. Rowland had limited influence over the day-to-day management of the football club.

The only way forward was to sell the individual units of Avon Inns. We were in the latter part of 1989; the financial crisis that would grip the early 1990s was beginning to pinch. Prices of commercial properties were falling and the 'assets' that had been dumped on me – with values that far inflated their worth – were locked into paying high rents.

However, I resolved not to allow any of this to affect my enjoyment of the forthcoming UEFA Cup tie. Royal Liege flew in and, while their team trained at Easter Road, the executives did their own thing, making use of the two hired limousines they had insisted we provide.

Among their party was a young midfielder whose name would become just as famous as any player on the continent. It is impossible today to write about the development of professional football without considering the impact of Jean-Marc Bosman. Having joined Royal Liege on a two-year deal in 1988, Bosman quickly fell out of favour and barely kicked a ball for the club. One of his rare appearances for them came in Edinburgh.

When his contract with Liege ended, at the end of the season, he agreed to sign for the French club Dunkerque. Liege refused to give up his registration. They claimed that although his contract had elapsed, he was still employed on a rollover basis. The club argued his employment with them would only end if he was sold for a fee or they decided to release him. Alternatively, he could sign a new deal on less than favourable terms. To underscore the division of power between club and player, Liege docked Bosman's wages by 75%.

Bosman brought a case against the Belgian FA and UEFA to the European Court of Justice, arguing he was being denied freedom of movement guaranteed under EU law. By the time the court ruled in his favour in 1995, the peak years of Bosman's career had been lost. The compensation he received barely covered his legal expenses, and he was later declared bankrupt. His legacy was the abolition of rules limiting the number of 'foreign' EU players clubs could field. It also guaranteed the principle of freedom of movement for players at the end of their contracts. Steve McManaman and Sol Campbell were two of the most high-profile British players to exploit the new rules. The pair made vast fortunes when moving on 'a Bosman' to Real Madrid and Arsenal respectively. Bosman had hoped players like them would support him by purchasing 'Who's the Boz?' t-shirts commissioned in recognition of the sacrifice he made on their behalf. The story goes that only one was ever sold, with the buyer said to be the son of Bosman's lawyer.

Royal Liege were mortally wounded by the Bosman affair, losing their stadium in 1995 as they battled to stave off insolvency. They would subsequently be dubbed "the homeless" by rival fans. Having merged with RFC Tilleur Saint-Nicolas, a diluted version of the club fell as far as the Belgian fourth tier. Long gone are the halcyon days of the 1980s when Royal Liege mixed it with Europe's elite.

This was all very much for the future when, on 18 October, 1989, pipers led the two teams onto the Easter Road pitch. Going into the game, Hibs had suffered only four defeats in 33 European home ties. A key ingredient in this record had always been the notorious Easter Road slope. If we won the toss, we would be sure to kick uphill in the first half and downhill in the second.

The kick-off was delayed by 15 minutes because of crowd congestion. But it was soon apparent that Liege had done their homework. Having won the toss, they turned the sides around. As we flew down the slope, roared on by a packed house, their aim was to frustrate us.

In truth, despite lots of possession, we struggled to create clear-cut chances in that first half. We did have one great opportunity to carry a lead with us to Belgium when Keith Houchen was brought down in the box. Houchie gathered the ball and stepped up to the spot – only to see his shot tipped brilliantly onto the post by the keeper. The second half was a largely uneventful slog, which ended goalless. My heart went out to Houchie who'd endured one of our fans shouting, "Houchen, if you'd had six free shots at John Lennon, he'd still be alive." Football fans can be cruel, and Keith was desperately upset after the game. His relationship with the supporters never really recovered. A year later, his Easter Road career ended on a sour note. Leaving the pitch after a poor performance, he aimed a V-sign at some Hibees who were giving him an earful.

Having failed to score an away goal, Liege left town in a hurry. Our optimism for the second leg, however, was dampened within a week. Aberdeen came to Easter Road and battered us 3-0. Fans were increasingly vocalising their discontent with both our league form and pragmatic style of play. They were right. We had stalled.

*

While the Tartan Army enjoys a long-standing and well-deserved glowing reputation abroad, in the 1980s Scottish club football was severely afflicted by incidents of hooliganism. Most clubs had a hooligan element in their following, and they were widely known as 'casuals'. The name referenced the fashion among these young men for wearing designer clothes to matches, rather than club colours. They would appear impeccably dressed until the fighting started – usually after the game in the town centre.

When I floated Hibernian, the *Sunday Sport*, owned by the current West Ham co-chairman David Sullivan, described me as "a champagne-guzzling casual". The article's headline was "Shocks and Scares". Hibs casuals were fearsome. Ridiculously, the paper had me as their leader. The nearest I ever came to committing football violence was taking a swing at the boardroom door, having once trapped my finger in it.

Now the most infamous Hibernian casual 'firm' was called the CCS (Capital City Service). Their mantra was "These colours don't run." While the complexities of travel to the Eastern Bloc had deterred the CCS from following us to Hungary in any numbers, Belgium was very much in striking distance. The prospect of trouble erupting on the streets of Liege hung over the entire trip.

The official party was booked into the best hotel in the city, but I was forced to miss the reception organised for us as I was fighting off a severe chest infection and wanted to rest ahead of the match. I probably shouldn't have travelled, but I really wanted to support Alex and the boys. Feeling a little better, I decided to venture out for a walk. There were Hibs fans everywhere I went. Liege is an industrial town, but the city centre is pretty. Sadly, the previous night it had been subjected to rampaging casuals who indiscriminately smashed up businesses.

Football club executives, following such incidents, are always at pains to convey that the majority of their fans are well behaved, and trouble-makers a tiny minority. That was true in Liege. But we knew as the match got underway, win or lose, we could expect little positive press. Hibs would return home in shame.

The game itself was end to end, full of excitement, and a very different spectacle to the first leg. If we could only find that away goal, Liege would be up against it. Andy Goram was giving a Man-of-the-Match performance, making a string of world-class saves. Just on the stroke of half-time, we lost Keith Houchen to injury. How he must have hated Liege. The two legs had not been kind to him. He was replaced by the young Pat McGinlay.

In the second half, if Goram was the star performer, Pat was a close second. The boy played his heart out. He scored a great 'goal' and, for 30 seconds, we were dreaming of a glamour tie in round three. Then the linesman's raised flag ruined everything. I doubt there has been a football book ever written that does not complain about how a poor decision turned a game. I am happy to perpetuate that particular literary tradition. Television replays would prove the goal should have stood. The linesman had been fooled by the speed of our attack.

With the tie locked at 0-0 after 180 minutes of football, the referee blew to indicate the start of extra time. I felt sure only a wonder goal could beat Goram on this night. Unfortunately, that's just what happened. An unstoppable shot from outside the area settled the match and brought our European adventure to an end. Our comfort was that we believed there would always be next year.

Entering our silent dressing room, the UEFA official indicated the two players he'd selected to provide random urine samples. It must have been a coincidence that our best performers, Andy and Pat, were selected. Andy was very dehydrated and could not give the sample immediately. He and Pat would have to remain in the changing room until the deed was done. As I was still feeling unwell, I agreed to keep them company while the others went to the dinner reception in town.

As the room emptied, Pat discreetly leant over and told me Andy could not give a sample. "I know, Pat," I said. "We'll just wait until he can." "No, chairman," replied Pat. "You don't understand, he CAN'T give a sample." My world collapsed as I realised the significance of what I was being told. Andy's career and reputation were in serious jeopardy. The club was in danger of losing a potential million-pound asset for who knew how long.

There was nothing to be done. Andy would have to fill the container eventually, and we would face the consequences together. I struck up a conversation with the German official. I discovered he was a hotelier from the Black Forest and followed this up by asking for a detailed account of his family history, schooling and swimming ribbons.

Eventually, Andy interrupted our chat to inform us that he had successfully peed in the pot. I do not know exactly how it happened but, due to a 'mix-up', the samples the official took away with him for analysis were both from the same source: Pat.

I would never condone cheating, and at this stage I did not even know if the test would show a performance-enhancing substance. Whatever Andy had taken, I was sure it would be founded in foolishness rather than malevolence. It was easy for me to say nothing because, at that time, I believed the sample was Andy's and the consequences inevitable. There was nothing to say. Of course, having later been apprised of the 'mix-up', I didn't think it appropriate to interfere.

In years to come, Andy would become a Rangers hero while Pat went to play at Parkhead. Very few who saw them line up against each other in the cauldron of an Old Firm derby would know the debt owed from one to the other.

When we returned from Liege, we had an immediate inquest. Andy was an honest man, which is why I never formed the view that he had deliberately cheated. His integrity was shown when he freely admitted to us that he had taken weight-reducing tablets. I do not know whether what he had taken was performance-enhancing. But as we had lost the tie, no harm had been done to Liege. Andy's lifestyle had always been challenging. And I am sure, as he put on weight, his only motivation in using these substances was to take it off again. As I have said, I had a genuine affection for Mr Goram, whom I thought to be a very kind, funny and inspirational man. Oh, and not to mention, one of the finest goalkeepers I have ever seen.

Later in his Rangers career, pictures emerged of Goram stood in front of an Ulster Volunteer Force flag. There were even rumours about him being friendly with the UVF commander Billy Wright, aka 'King Rat'. Understandably, many Hibs fans were offended by this – to say the least. I reflected on all my dealings with Andy. His loyalty to Hibs had never been in question. The way I saw it, once he'd joined Rangers, he would commit to the Ibrox cause with equal passion. Unfortunately, in Glasgow, his naivety, eagerness to please people and fondness for a drink led him down some unedifying paths. I can't imagine he ever intentionally set out to offend our supporters. That isn't who he was. The Andy Goram I knew didn't give a damn about sectarianism and bigotry. He was too busy having fun.

With our European adventure over, the harsh reality of our domestic form caused me increasing concern. It was only November, but we were already way off the pace in the league. We had also been eliminated from the League Cup in the early rounds – a competition I'd hoped we might win – losing at home to Dunfermline.

Things were gloomy back in London too. I'd been summoned for another meeting at the Serious Fraud Office. While Les Marston and his associates remained the subject of the investigation, the SFO now asked me what I knew about David Rowland's affairs.

The transfer of properties to his INOCO firm, through the shell company Dutch Klinker, (registered in the Netherlands), certainly gave David a massive tax advantage. But it was perfectly legal, provided the structure wasn't solely set up to evade tax. It comes down to intent and, when you employ the best City lawyers and one of the top five accountancy companies, bad intentions become very difficult to prove. Rowland had never discussed his tax affairs with me. Even if I had wanted to, I could offer the SFO very little help.

I had a complicated relationship with Rowland from a legal perspective. On the one hand, as my client, some of what I knew about him fell within the regulations governing solicitor-client confidentiality. On the other, he was my business partner, and what I learned from that relationship had no legal privilege.

It seemed possible that David was spending more days in the UK than his tax-advantageous 'non-dom' status permitted. UK domiciles pay UK tax on all their worldwide earnings. If, however, you are domiciled offshore, you only have to pay UK tax on earnings made within the UK. Then there were my lingering concerns about who exactly owned some of the shares in Hibs.

As I couldn't answer the SFO investigator's questions about Rowland beyond offering them a perfunctory "I don't know" or "that is privileged", a sickening realisation dawned on me. These men weren't just interested in Marston and Rowland. They could now be after me too.

Following this meeting, I was told not to inform Rowland of the SFO's enquiries. I complied with this instruction. I did, however, tell Jeremy James, assuming that he would faithfully report it to Rowland himself.

In the time that I knew him, whenever his affairs came under the spotlight, I never found David Rowland to be fazed in the slightest.

TWELVE

A LONG WAY FROM HOME

AS OTTÓ HAD predicted, the pace of change behind the Iron Curtain was rapid. In line with the new convivial relationship between Thatcher and Gorbachev, Britain looked for opportunities in the East. To support this aim, a grand exhibition was to be held in Ukraine, imaginatively called 'Britain in Kiev'. The showcase aspired to be far more than a bog-standard trade fair. The plans included a football match between the great Dynamo Kiev and a yet-to-be-determined British team. Most strikingly of all, the RAF's Red Arrows were going to be invited into the Soviet Union's airspace to perform a flyover of Kiev, an act unthinkable just months before.

The civil servant charged with delivering 'Britain in Kiev' was Sir Curtis Keeble, the father of my dear friend and colleague, Jane. Sir Curtis – who had advised me ahead of my meetings with the SFO – asked if Hibs would be interested in participating in the project scheduled for the summer of 1990. Jim and I met Sir Curtis at his dusty, old office close to Buckingham Palace to arrange the match. We agreed to take the team to Kiev and represent Great Britain in a symbolically important fixture.

With hindsight, I believe, rather than extending a hand of friendship to the ailing USSR, Mrs Thatcher had a very different agenda for Britain in Kiev. She was hoping to steal a march in establishing a trading relationship with the soon to be sovereign state of Ukraine.

Sir Curtis asked if we could go out to the Soviet Union. There were people he wanted us to meet both in Moscow and the Ukrainian capital. My legal office was entrusted with the daunting task of arranging the trip. Visas for the USSR were issued for specific set dates. Only those who could provide an itinerary of how they intended to spend every minute of their stay had any chance of their application being approved. I formed the impression that the Soviet embassy revelled in its reputation for slowness and excessive bureaucracy. When we were eventually issued a visa, the dates did not tally with our request. The flight bookings and accommodation arrangements we'd made were now useless.

This had already happened once before and I couldn't bear repeating the whole rigmarole again. I decided not to notice the discrepancy nor tell Jim, reasoning that if the authorities did not like our papers, they would bar us from entering the plane. We were booked on the Aeroflot to Moscow, where we had two nights before an internal flight to Kiev.

On arrival, it was clear there were two contrasting Moscows. The first was what the authorities allowed the Western world to see on television and in the press; vast stadiums and marvellous buildings, especially around Red Square. The second Moscow was kept secret. Bleak concrete tower blocks, food queues and massive saloons in the hotels, full of one-armed bandits and lines of people anxious to gamble a few coins.

We stayed at the Intourist Hotel, where every floor had a 24-hour reception. My sense was their role was to monitor their guests' activity more than provide a warm welcome. We visited the usual tourist stops in the daytime, Lenin's Mausoleum, the Kremlin and Saint Basil's Cathedral. At night, we drank beer in a deserted cocktail bar where the staff tersely refused payment in roubles and insisted on American dollars.

The contacts we had arranged to meet in Moscow before moving on to Kiev proved much friendlier. We had our picture taken with a few young soldiers at the entrance to Gorky Park. All smiling. The park was referenced in the Scorpions' song 'Winds of Change', which a year later became an anthem for those celebrating the collapse of the Eastern Bloc. Whenever I've heard the song since, I've always pictured those soldiers' smiling faces.

When it was time to fly to Kiev, we were taken to a different airport. Inside, we were struck by the fact that there were only a handful of other passengers and that none of them were Russians. As I peered out of the window, I was confronted by dozens of planes (all Tupolevs). My curiosity was now piqued: why so many planes for so few passengers?

Jim and I decided to explore and left the terminal. We were immediately followed by a young man, who had been a recurring character – always several paces behind us – throughout our mission to Moscow. Our tail surely must have quickly realised neither Jim nor I was 007. Nonetheless, orders were doubtless orders, and the poor fella had to continue to follow us until we boarded the plane and became someone else's problem. We moved on to another large building in the airport. Opening the door, we were taken aback to find an alternative departure hall packed with people and row upon row of gambling machines. One of the games required the player to manoeuvre a miniature crane to win prizes. Among the rewards was a bar of soap.

It was clear that the airport was designed to keep foreigners and natives as strictly segregated as the Old Firm on derby day. Indeed, we were first on the plane and given berths at the front.

After a while, other passengers began to board, and they all had to walk past us to their seats. It was an incredible spectacle to behold. One man's carry-on consisted of a live duck. Another had a piglet in a cage. There seemed to be no limit to how much luggage passengers were allowed. I began to wonder how, with all this extra weight, the plane would get off the ground.

I have never before or since had such a scary flight. The pilot had left the cockpit door open. As an aviator myself, I immediately recognised the international warning of a potential engine stall that he was broadcasting to the tower. We could not have been more than 5,000 feet into take-off when the captain levelled off to gain momentum. I could have kissed him when we touched down safely in Kiev. I vowed as the wheels hit the tarmac that for our return with Hibs in the summer, only a Western charter flying direct to Ukraine's capital would do.

*

First on our to-do list in communist Kiev was finding a taxi firm that could provide us with a driver for the duration of our stay. With hard currency in our pockets, we didn't have to enquire for long. Marcus, speaking perfect English, agreed to be our guide and wheelman.

Kiev is a beautiful city that, at the time, had a population of around 2.5 million. However, the cracks in the once rock-solid Soviet system were by now increasingly apparent on the weary people's faces. On one occasion, I stopped to buy a Coke from a machine outside a bakery. There was a long queue waiting for bread. The vending machine only took dollars, which few local people had. Trying to treat a young boy in the line, I bought him a bottle. Rather than drinking it, he instead gave it to his mother. I presume she then used it to barter for essentials.

The city wore the scars of the terrible events of 26 April, 1986, when reactor four at the Chernobyl Nuclear Power Plant fractured and exploded. Kiev was a mere 60 miles from the plant.

Our hotel bedrooms overlooked the Dynamo Stadium, a massive 70,000-seat arena, and home to one of Europe's truly great teams. Marcus told us that the stadium was filled for every Dynamo game. Alongside it was a ski-jump, which seemed to end just outside our hotel window.

After we'd checked in, Marcus suggested that he take us to the best restaurant in town for lunch. He showed us into a large dining room, where a trio of musicians played beautiful music. The menu, which was in English, came in an old leather-bound folder and carried an extensive wine list. We ordered our starter and main course, but were immediately told by the waiter that none of our choices were available.

Rather than selecting alternatives, we were informed it would be easier if he told us what was being served today. The 'choice' was pork and vegetables with a generous measure of vodka to wash it down. Nevertheless, so good did the food prove to be that we returned there for lunch every day of our visit.

The following morning, while Jim attended to some other business I met the Dynamo Kiev officials at Dynamo Stadium. There to greet me was the most celebrated Soviet footballer of them all, Lev Yashin. My mind instantly took me back to my first visit to Upton Park as a 13-year-old. Those were the days when West Ham had Bobby Moore, Geoff Hurst and Martin Peters. They had also just signed the Scotland international Bobby Ferguson for £65,000 – a reportedly record fee for a goalkeeper in those days. I remembered that the Hammers fans had a song that started, "Aye-aye, aye-aye, Ferguson's better than Yashin." I told Lev that such was his reputation his name had even been sung in far-away England.

I knew that the world's best-ever number 1 had spent his entire playing career at Dynamo Moscow and now acted as an ambassador for that club. It was curious, therefore, to see him here at the headquarters of Dynamo Kiev. Lev was unquestionably a committed Soviet, so presumably his presence was designed to impress me. If that was the case, the authorities could consider that box firmly ticked.

Sadly, Lev was very ill. He had lost a leg a few years before and was now suffering from cancer. Soon after we returned from Kiev, the world read of his passing, taken far too soon, aged just 60. I was fortunate to meet some incredible people through Hibs and made some wonderful friends. In all humility, the most impressive person I ever met was the dying 'Black Spider', as Yashin was widely known.

Outside Dynamo Stadium, my eyes were drawn to a striking statue. Through an interpreter, Lev told me the story it commemorated. On 9 August, 1942, while the city was under Nazi occupation, Kiev hosted what has become known as the 'Death Match'. A crowd of some 2,000 spectators is believed to have watched FC Start – a team comprised of former Dynamo Kiev players turned bakers – take on the German military side Flakelf. The events that occurred after Start's 5-3 victory have become the stuff of myth and legend. Yashin relayed the official Soviet account to me. All the victorious Ukrainian players, he said, were immediately hauled from the pitch and executed.

When it was time for us to go, Lev generously said that he looked forward to meeting the Hibs players and was excited at the prospect of watching us play in Kiev. Our final day in Ukraine was far less memorable as we thrashed out the arrangements for the team's visit. That evening, I heard lots of noise coming from the hotel's function room. Always on the lookout for a good time at the end of a long day's work, I made a break for the door. Within seconds of breaching this forbidden zone, I found myself being escorted back to the sterile 'dollar' bar by the polite but firm staff.

We did, at least, get one last chance to mix with the local people when we headed back to the vodka and pork restaurant for dinner. It was much busier than it had been during the day. Upon hearing our accents, one young man approached me and urged that I take his sister back to Scotland and marry her. She was both beautiful and desperate for an escape, but there was nothing I could do to help her.

In the morning, I went to the hotel reception to collect our passports for the flight home. It was a standard requirement in the Eastern Bloc that these be handed over for safekeeping when you first arrived. "Mr Duff," said the Intourist rep, "we have big problem. Your visa has expired." Panicked, he immediately tried to contact the authorities in Moscow.

My silent prayer that the communication system would fail was answered. He couldn't find a working telephone line between the cities. Reluctantly, the rep agreed to release our passports on the condition that I report to the security personnel at the airport in Moscow. We flew back to the Russian capital, 'forgetting' this instruction and, much to my relief, were allowed to board our flight home.

We had travelled to the USSR without valid visas and I had met Lev Yashin. It was a risk I'd repeat in a heartbeat. I couldn't wait to see our players line up against the great Dynamo when we returned in the summer.

But unfortunately, unbeknown to me, our plans for Hibs to play a starring role for Britain in Kiev were soon to be scuppered by Wallace Mercer.

THIRTEEN

THE FORWARD PLAN

AS THE 1989/90 season progressed, I started to share the view held by many of our fans: Alex Miller was struggling. If he could not take us any further forward, he would need to be replaced. I began to consider potential options. Joe Jordan was a fearsome striker who had played with distinction for Leeds, Manchester United and AC Milan. His lack of front teeth had earned him the nickname Jaws. He was a prolific goal-scorer and had won the first of his many Scotland caps while I was still a teenager. Jordan was at the time the manager of Bristol City. I could easily make an approach without alerting the Scottish newspapers. We arranged to have dinner at a hotel in Bath. Feeling each other out, we exchanged football stories before getting down to the Hibs job.

I found Joe to be a quiet, considered and intelligent man. We agreed to meet again, and Joe was very much in line to take over should we have decided to call time on Alex. Neither side had committed totally, but both parties had expressed their interest. Had matters not overtaken us, I am pretty sure he would have been the next Hibs manager. As fate would have it, following the harrowing events of the summer of 1990, Jordan became the new incumbent of the Tynecastle dugout. I think the appointment may have been one final piece of one-upmanship at my expense by Wallace Mercer.

We started 1990 in inauspicious fashion, losing 2-0 at Tynecastle on New Year's Day. But, as painful as this result was to take, it proved a mere scratch compared to the deep wounds those in the Hearts boardroom would soon inflict upon us.

With the team struggling, Alex decided to leave out Archie for our trip to Motherwell. When Archie saw he'd been omitted from the team sheet, he stormed out of the dressing room and hailed a taxi from outside Fir Park to take him back to Edinburgh. The fallout was so bad that Archie demanded to be released from the remainder of his contract. He moved back to Barcelona, where he signed for Espanyol. I was gutted to see him go. Even though Archie's time at Easter Road ended acrimoniously, I'll always cherish that winning moment he gave us the season before at Tynecastle.

Defeats at home to St Mirren and away to Dundee later in the month, where again we failed to score, led me further to question Alex Miller's position. Did he have a future with the club? As I peered gloomily out of the coach window on the journey back from Dens Park, John Collins sidled up to me and said, "Cheer up, chairman. We're going to win the Tennents' Soccer Sixes [due to start the following day], and I'll give you the match ball from the final when we do." John was never the type to make such bold claims, so he must have been genuinely worried about my wellbeing to have said this to me. In truth, I had forgotten all about the two-day, six-a-side tournament held at the Scottish Exhibition and Conference Centre in Glasgow. It seems incredible now, but this event took place annually from 1984 to 1993 – right in the busiest period of the domestic football season.

All the Premier Division clubs would send their first-team squads and the tournament was keenly contested by the players

– not least because it was screened on STV and came with a tidy £16,000 prize fund divided up among the winning squad.

As ever for a trip to Glasgow, our team bus departed Easter Road with those players who resided around Leith on board. Those who lived in the west of the city would flag the coach down from a bus stop at the Maybury, where they stood shivering in a gaggle of green tracksuits. For the 'Sixes', the clubs would wear the same kit they wore in first-team games. But for some inexplicable reason, no players wore shin pads. I think there was some sort of gentlemen's agreement between the teams that they would not go in too hard. Inevitably this went out of the window as soon as the group-stage games kicked off. Even though the playing surface was allegedly Astroturf – it looked more like green sandpaper to me – players launched into challenges full force. The pitch was surrounded by perspex screens, meaning the ball hardly ever went out of play. This only added to the intensity of the matches as behemoths like St Mirren's Peter Godfrey flattened our players against the walls.

We were in a pool with Dundee, Dundee United, Rangers and Godfrey's Saints. The 'Sixes' format saw any drawn games decided on penalties, even in the round-robin. The top two teams from the groups would advance to the semi-finals and final, played the next day. Goram and Paul Kane were outstanding in the group-stage games. Kano had played most of the season at right-back. But in the 'Sixes', he was deployed up top and showed just what a quality footballer he was. He scored a hat-trick as we demolished Dundee United 5-1, both our goals in a 2-0 win over St Mirren and another in a 2-0 win over Dundee. These wins, combined with a shootout victory over Rangers after a 0-0 draw, saw us advance to a semi-final against Hearts.

A capacity crowd of 7,000 created one of the best atmospheres I've ever encountered in football. It was clear how badly our players wanted to win it for the Hibees who had travelled over to Glasgow. In a tight match, Hearts took the lead in the second half through Tosh McKinlay, who powered a low shot past Goram. With the semi-finals consisting of 10-minute halves, we didn't have long to respond to falling behind. As the clock ticked down, John Collins was a man on a mission. He won possession in the Hearts half, tackling away at a defender he'd pinned in the corner as if he was chopping down an oak tree. The ball suddenly popped free, and John played a perfect ball across the box for Kano to slot home our equaliser.

With no further goals, the raucous crowd counted down the final 10 seconds of the match. The buzzer sounded, taking the tie to an abridged penalty shootout of four spot-kicks each. Young Scott Crabbe, whose flowing hair somehow still looked like it had just been blow-dried, stepped up first for Hearts and blasted the ball past Andy. Paul Kane then saw his effort down the middle well saved by Henry Smith. I can only imagine Kano was distracted by the outrageous maroon tracksuit bottoms sported by big Henry – no doubt worn to guard against friction burns. Thankfully, Tosh McKinlay crashed Hearts' second penalty against the bar, leaving Pat McGinlay to level things up.

John Robertson went next for the Jambos. His effort was brilliantly saved by Andy. In truth, our number 1 had come so far off his line to narrow the angle he almost reached the ball before Robertson had struck it. I think the referee was caught up in all the excitement, and we certainly weren't complaining when he didn't order a re-take. Given that players took their run-ups from the halfway line – before absolutely battering the ball from a penalty spot no more than eight yards from the goal – it's a wonder there was never a goalkeeping fatality at the 'Sixes'. Alan Sneddon failed to take advantage with our third kick, again shooting straight at Henry Smith. Goram, however, was in no mood to lose to Hearts. From the next kick, he made a great stop with his legs to deny Gary Mackay. Finally, John Collins spotted up the ball with a chance to send us through to the final. It was never in doubt. His precise strike arrowed into the bottom left corner.

The other semi-final was also decided on penalties. St Mirren triumphed over Motherwell to set up a reunion between us and our old friend Peter Godfrey. Having played our semi first, we had more time to recuperate than the Buddies, and it showed. The main obstacle we had to overcome was the literal fridge they had in goal. The fantastically named Les Fridge had been superb in our group-stage match with them. He was again in good form in the final, but could do little when Kano jumped for a Neil Cooper cross and headed us in front in the first half. That was Kane's eighth goal of the competition – securing him the golden boot.

St Mirren included a young Paul Lambert in their side who was emerging as one of the best midfielders in Scotland that season. It came as no surprise that he went on to have such a decorated career with Borussia Dortmund and Celtic. However, in the final, John Collins dominated both Lambert and Billy Davies in the midfield battle.

It was John who secured the cup, doubling our lead in the second half. A lovely little shimmy saw him shift the ball onto his left foot, engineering the half-yard he needed to shoot through Les Fridge's legs. Just as he'd promised, after the full-time buzzer sounded confirming our victory, John handed me the fluorescent-yellow Adidas Tango ball. I still cherish it to this day. Of course, the Tennents' Sixes wasn't the Scottish Cup or Premier Division title, but it was the first piece of silverware for the Easter Road trophy cabinet since the 1973 Drybrough Cup final triumph over Celtic. I was particularly thrilled for Paul Kane, who was such a terrific player during his eight years at Hibs. Kano was an Edinburgh boy, and I remember him once telling me his dad first took him to a match at Easter Road when he was only two. Paul now heads up the association for former players. A proper Hibee through and through.

As we celebrated, someone pointed out that the Hearts players and staff hadn't stayed behind to watch the final. We didn't miss them.

Sometime in the weeks after our triumph in the 'Sixes', the local Merchant School had an open day. My children were approaching the age when they would soon be joining as pupils there. Given what was to come that summer, it is one of life's incredible coincidences that I was shown around by Wallace Mercer's son. He was a very polite and friendly young man. When I told him who I was, he innocently said something to the effect that his dad was going to buy Hibs. I gently set him straight: "Don't think so, son."

At the time, I thought absolutely nothing of it. Only after Wallace's bid came in did I realise the significance of this little exchange. And despite what was subsequently speculated in the press, that was the only clue I ever got of his plan.

*

With Hibs due to play in Kiev and Scotland sealing qualification for the World Cup in Italy, the summer of 1990 promised to be a belter. I was planning to take in the Scotland games by flying my own single-engine plane to Genoa and Turin. Maybe I'd even make it to Bari if we progressed beyond the group stage for the first time. The saying goes, when we are sure of exactly what we'll do, the angels laugh. They were soon to be in hysterics.

Hibs' season ended in bitter disappointment. Eliminated in the quarter-final of the Scottish Cup by Dundee United, our only chance of qualifying for Europe was via the league. Our final three games of the season all looked winnable, and we were odds-on to seal fourth place and a route back into the UEFA Cup. But crushingly, we managed to garner just two points from those fixtures and dropped to a final position of seventh. Celtic and Motherwell were only above us on goal difference, and Dundee United, who crept into the final European spot, were a solitary point better off. Alex's aversion to attacking football and the falling out with Archie had cost us dearly.

More hurtful still, Hearts had finished third. I always believed that the existence of two strong teams in Edinburgh was good for the city, but that was on the proviso that we weren't left looking up at them.

At Avon Inns, turnover was slightly up, and prospects marginally better. But with rising interest rates, the debt was still crippling. The bleak financial climate also meant the Frank Graham Group were struggling. They wanted out of the shirt sponsorship deal, or at the very least to delay the payment for the next season, which would soon be due. We couldn't agree to scrap a deal we'd entered into in good faith, but I was prepared to reschedule their instalments.

Against this backdrop, I had begun formulating two possible tracks to keep my Hibs dream alive. Both would see David Rowland removed from my life. Our partnership had reached a breaking point when I defied his directive that we sign no further players.

Young Mark McGraw, at Morton, was courting interest from top clubs both north and south of the border as a promising forward. Liverpool and Rangers were regularly sending scouts to watch him. His father Allan was the manager at Morton and had himself played for Hibs. He was keen for his son to progress his career at Easter Road and agreed to what we thought was a bargain at a modest £200,000. Unfortunately, McGraw the younger never made the grade, scoring only a handful of goals for the club during several injury-blighted seasons.

Rowland was livid and gave me both foul-mouthed barrels. I replied in kind. I have no idea whether he was already talking to Wallace Mercer by this stage. But I am sure this latest conflict between us was the catalyst for him deciding to cut ties with Hibs. I had gambled that McGraw would see us over the line for European qualification. It was a mistake for which I, as the chairman signing the cheques, was ultimately responsible. But my focus right until the bitter end was to create a successful Hibs team on the park.

One way or another now, Rowland had to go. The question for me was, could I find a way to stay on without him?

*

The media told us Michael Knighton did not have the money to honour his agreement to buy Manchester United. When he'd made his bid in August 1989 – complete with his keepy-uppy routine – he did have private funding in place and a business partner. Within a short time, this had fallen apart. I decided to travel to Manchester and visit Martin Edwards. I had the seeds of a plan to use Martin's difficulties with Knighton to perhaps extract Rowland from Hibs at a price that would stabilise the club again.

The chairman's office at Old Trafford is like no other. Accessed through the main entrance, under the stand by the railway line, the elevator to the top floor gave no clue to the opulence I found within. Martin Edwards' 'office' was more akin to a luxury apartment. The premier feature – revealed with a twist of the blinds – was a giant, one-way window, offering a panoramic view of British football's most famous pitch.

My plan was simple. If Knighton was not going to buy Manchester United, maybe I could broker a deal between Edwards and Rowland. My commission would allow me the working capital I needed to take the club I loved forward.

Martin Edwards had inherited United from his father, Louis. Edwards senior, a Manchester butcher, had first joined the

United board the day after the Munich air disaster in 1958. The patriarch of the Edwards family had carefully cultivated an image of the Salford boy made good, and was known throughout the game as 'Champagne Louis'. In 1980, however, the respected documentary team at World in Action revealed some grimy business at the Theatre of Dreams. The programme triggered a police inquiry. The butcher was for the chop.

The allegations involved illegal share deals with hefty cash payments and illicit inducements to entice players. Peter Lorimer's parents were allegedly offered several thousand pounds in an attempt to sway the youngster to sign for Manchester United instead of Leeds. A matter of weeks after the television exposé, Louis Edwards passed away from a heart attack.

My sense was that Martin, having seen the damaging spotlight the Old Trafford chairmanship had shone on his father, was keen to avoid similar scrutiny. He was coming under increasing fire from the United fans, disgruntled by a lack of progress on the pitch in the early years of Alex Ferguson's reign.

On my visits to see Martin, we would sometimes have lunch in the club restaurant. Every time I was there, I would see Matt Busby and his wife. Sir Matt was football royalty, but it seemed to me Martin was uncomfortable with the respect and love engendered by the great man.

One of the first questions I asked Martin was how the Knighton deal had come about. The answer was astonishing. Apparently, Martin had a massive unsecured overdraft. His personal and corporate financiers had always been relaxed about this. But suddenly, someone further up the banking chain of command instructed the local fund manager to gain some security from Martin.

By profound coincidence, the same day that Martin received the bank's request for security, he also took a telephone call from a go-between acting for Michael Knighton. Knighton offered to buy Edwards' shares and cover the cost of rebuilding Old Trafford's outdated Stretford End. Edwards did not know Knighton, but unsettled by the bank's change of tone, assumed the offer to be somehow connected. There and then, he decided to sell the club. He had received offers in the past, but it was the timing of Knighton's approach that proved decisive.

To this very day, Knighton considers himself a visionary. In reality, however, the saga of his takeover bid for Manchester United was a farce. Knighton's main backer was Stanley Cohen who, with his business partner Bob Thornton – the former chairman of Debenhams – would produce the funding to buy the club. Knighton told me directly that he had shaken hands on a 50-50 agreement with them. Seeing that Knighton was on the verge of pulling off the deal, Cohen changed the terms to 60-40 in his own favour. Knighton refused to accept this and consequently lost his funding.

Had he agreed to the new deal offered by his erstwhile partner Cohen, he might have been the Manchester United chairman for many years. Knighton, however, yet to pay a penny, believed United already belonged to him. In the currencies of self-confidence and audacity, Michael Knighton was rich beyond his wildest dreams.

Although Knighton is a Yorkshireman, who ran a posh school in the county, he boasted serious Scottish connections. His home was a windy castle on the west coast, a short drive from Donald Trump's golf course at Turnberry. I once had tea there and had to keep my coat on to prevent hypothermia. His wife belonged to Edinburgh's famous Croan family. They had made their fortune in the seafood business. Their company's headquarters were just around the corner from where I'd attended primary school.

It was, therefore, not surprising that having lost his backing, and with time being of the essence, Knighton looked to Scotland for a new source of funding for his Manchester United deal. Enter stage left, Gavin Masterton and David Murray. Soon rumours began to swirl. Apparently, a syndicate of Scottish businessmen had come forward, trying to shore up Knighton's bid. I believe they came within hours of pulling it off. Had it gone through, my best guess is that David Murray would have eventually left Rangers and installed himself at Old Trafford. I can say with authority that neither the FA nor the SFA would have allowed Murray to officially own or part-own both clubs.

Certainly, Knighton was to be the syndicate's first chairman of United. That was the most important aspect to him. His pride would accept nothing less. Nevertheless, notwithstanding whose name would have been on the door, Murray and Masterton would unquestionably have been the dominant influences in Manchester.

Knighton travelled to meet with Murray and Masterton shortly after losing his original backing. The negotiations were hard fought, but a deal was eventually hammered out. The sticking point was that bank rules bound Knighton to offer personal guarantees. He was not keen to risk his castle and school. What Masterton and the Bank of Scotland would gain from a deal involving Knighton remains a matter of much speculation.

Knighton eventually yielded to the demand for personal securities and the parties adjourned. The agreement was ready to sign the following afternoon. Privately, however, Knighton was having second thoughts and mentioned this to his advisers. One of them came forward at this point to say they knew of another potential financier. The alternative backer, they assured him, would not demand any securities. This way, Knighton would be able to take the helm at United with no personal risk.

After a series of calls, the Knighton party, unbeknown to Murray or Masterton, decided to ask for a meeting. The man in question, Eddy Shah, was the founder of the *Today* newspaper.

Rather than Shah giving Knighton the money he needed, instead Knighton was skewered in the tabloids. Suddenly the papers were awash with stories alleging United's purported new owner was skint. One even jested Knighton was so impoverished that his mother-in-law had taken to sending him down food parcels from Scotland.

Mortally wounded, Knighton frantically tried to revive his agreement with Murray and Masterton. But there was to be no way back. At Old Trafford, Martin Edwards read the headlines with a sinking feeling. The debacle of his dalliance with Knighton had been exposed to the world. Far from solving all his problems, Michael Knighton had turned Edwards, and the great Manchester United, into a laughing stock.

As I began meeting Martin in the first half of 1990, Knighton was still hanging around Old Trafford, having been invited to join the board despite his failure to complete a deal. It made no sense.

But Edwards could not simply cut his ties with Knighton, as he explained to me. "I've made the mistake of telling Knighton where the Manchester United bodies are buried." Having been roughed up repeatedly in the press, Edwards admitted to me he was running scared. You did not need to be an expert to understand that had Knighton been able to produce the funds, he would have struck football's deal of the century.

Seeing that he was desperate to be shot of the whole embarrassing affair, I offered to broker an alternative sale for Martin at a little less than what Knighton had offered. Martin agreed. I suppose I was not very different from Knighton in the sense that I did not have the money to buy the club myself. Unlike him, however, I did know several people, David Rowland among them, who could – and probably would – buy Manchester United if I could tee up a deal on their behalf. Also, based on my travails playing in the Hibs Legends team, there was no way that I'd be seeking publicity by ball juggling on the pitch!

Robert Maxwell would have been the obvious solution, but relations between the two men were toxic. Edwards had rebuffed Maxwell's bid for the club in the mid-1980s, and Maxwell had used his newspapers to take shots at the United chairman ever since. Unfortunately for Martin, there was no shortage of ammunition: alleged affairs and tax irregularities were tabloid manna from heaven. Nothing I read in the *Daily Mirror* surprised me.

On my fourth visit to United, Martin insisted I stay until the morning and be a judge in the 'Miss Manchester United' competition. He took me to a function room, where the contestants were rehearsing. I had no idea how I would choose who would win the crown. I need not have fretted as, when we left, Martin told me that contestant number six would be victorious. It was all an elaborate charade designed to honour his then-girlfriend.

After this sham, we talked about Alex Ferguson. There has always been debate over whether the great man really was one defeat from losing his job in the 1989/90 season. I can confirm Martin Edwards told me that had United lost to Nottingham Forest in the FA Cup third round, a change would have been made. Who knows, maybe we could have persuaded Alex to join his brother at Hibs.

I can also attest that, despite speculation over the years, Martin Edwards never considered appointing Brian Clough manager at Old Trafford. There was a long-standing antipathy between Clough and the United board. One of Clough's final acts as Derby manager had been to aim a V-sign at Louis Edwards and Sir Matt Busby across the Old Trafford directors' box. The United directors had long memories. Martin opined Clough's pointed digs at Manchester United in the press stemmed from bitterness that the club had never come calling for his services.

Martin once told me a story of a game at Old Trafford when Clough's Forest were the visitors. After the match, which United won, Clough was unhappy with his team's performance, not least that of his son Nigel. Clough asked Martin if he would "do him the honour of coming down to the visitors' dressing room to be introduced to Nigel". Martin was confused. He already knew the Forest number 9, who by this time was an England international. When the two men reached the away dressing room, Nigel was combing his hair in the mirror.

"Nigel," said his father, "this is Martin Edwards, chairman of a great football club."

"Martin, this is Nigel."

As the two shook hands, Brian turned to leave. From the corridor came that unmistakable voice: "By the way, Nigel, he thinks you're crap too." Such was the humour and cruelty of the man.

Keen to get home and recount these great tales to Jim, before the end of my trip, Martin introduced me to a few members of the United board. I shook hands and chatted about my plans with Amer Al Midani, a dapper businessman from Beirut, Maurice Watkins, the club's solicitor, and one of its legends, Bobby Charlton.

As with Knighton's bid, timing is everything. Had I known Rowland was lining up a deal with Mercer to get out of Hibs, I would have gone straight to him with the United proposal as soon as I knew it was feasible. The modern history of both Hibs and Manchester United might have worked out very differently if I had. Instead, I was cautious. I needed to tie myself in on an option agreement with Martin, but events in Edinburgh were soon to overwhelm me.

As well as United's run to the 1990 FA Cup final saving Alex Ferguson, it may well have spared Martin Edwards. Jim and I were his guests at the replay of the final against Crystal Palace.

United won 1–0. It was to prove the first of many trophies during the Ferguson–Edwards era.

At the old Wembley, the official party were able to stand outside on a balcony, facing Wembley Way. There, among the United directors and dignitaries who were waving down to the club's fans, stood Michael Knighton, soaking up what he thought to be the glory of his club. The problem was, the fans were actually shaking fists and shouting pithy phrases along the lines of "Fuck off, Knighton!" In the end, Martin Edwards had to usher him away from the balcony as more fans shouted abuse. Little did they know that it was impossible to insult the man. Michael Knighton lived on Planet Knighton, and there he made the rules.

The football world knows that eventually Knighton 'bought' Carlisle United, where he dispensed with the usual structures of a football club and appointed himself both chairman and manager. I believe Knighton is writing his own book about his time at Carlisle. It will make a fascinating read, no doubt. I wait with interest to discover whether it confirms what Martin Edwards told me: that he helped Knighton buy Carlisle to get him out of Old Trafford.

A year on from that FA Cup triumph, Edwards successfully floated Manchester United on the stock exchange and made a fortune.

*

My second plan to offload Rowland and take Hibs to the next level centred on moving the club from Leith. Hibs had six acres of surplus stadium ground, which extended just off Easter Road – almost to where the Meadowbank retail park is now. The land had vast potential residential development value. I believed if this land was harnessed to the benefit of the club in combination with a new stadium built on Edinburgh's outskirts, Hibernian's future would be gilded for generations to come. Regrettably, things did not play out that way.

My view was that taking the stadium out of town would produce capital and income for the club and cover the expense of building a brand-new all-seater ground. The recommendations of the Taylor Report, published in January 1990 in the wake of the Hillsborough disaster, meant that Scottish top-flight clubs would need to develop all-seater stadiums. We began to explore our options. Only now, all these years later, have I come to comprehend how the Taylor Report, the grants on offer to assist clubs in complying with its recommendations and the possibility of leveraging the need for new stadiums to unlock green-belt land for commercial development all proved powerful stimuli to those behind the Edinburgh United plot.

The architect Grant Butchart – despite being relatively unknown – was one of Edinburgh's power brokers. He predominantly lived in Belgravia, London, next to the German Embassy. But he also owned a lovely home in Edinburgh, with what looked to be more than an acre of mature garden. The house was reached from a private drive at Canaan Lane, in well-to-do Morningside, and could not be seen from the road. His favourite 'toy' was a red Ferrari that he was fond of taking on midnight drives at breakneck speed around the country roads to the south of the city.

Butchart had been instrumental in moving St Johnstone to their new stadium, McDiarmid Park, which opened in August 1989 and made him a tidy sum in the process. The value of a deal to relocate Hibs would be worth far, far more. Butchart began making overtures to me.

Just off the Edinburgh bypass, beyond the city limits, lies a place called Straiton. The area had been home to the Bilston Glen Colliery, but in 1989 the mine was closed, the latest victim of Margaret Thatcher's brutal war with the miners. Straiton already had a small retail park, set some way back from the main road and up a hill. The rest of the surrounding land was empty. Ripe for development. Across the main road sat a pub and some chalets. Butchart had identified Straiton as the ideal site to house a New Easter Road.

We began working very closely on the project, having regular exploratory meetings in London and Edinburgh. I found it impossible to place Grant. He was a very secretive man. Much of what I subsequently learned of him came from my observation and information gleaned from his family.

The development would be delivered by a newly formed company that was to be a partnership of Hibernian Football Club and Grant Butchart.

Such a deal would be worth tens of millions. Beyond a prospective boost in the value of Edinburgh Hibernian PLC shares, I did not stand to make any money personally from the Straiton development. However, such was the transformative potential of Straiton for Hibs that, I believe, had the project come off, not every league title since 1985 would have gone to Glasgow.

With Hibernian on board, there would still be plenty more land to develop and potential profits for the club to share in. Along the back of the site, there was a potential for residential housing. We felt sure that including a football stadium in a green-belt redevelopment project made it very attractive to the planning authorities. Hibs' involvement would likely make the difference in unlocking the whole site for retail. Butchart was already in discussions with a supermarket about the possibility of opening a Straiton superstore.

I was never secretive about Straiton. I remember posing for a photo at the site with a Hibernian football. I expressed my opinion that inner-city stadiums had seen their day. I reasoned that the plan would gain support from the city council, tourism board and retailers. They would all be happy to see casuals diverted away from the centre of town on match days.

We honed our plans and knew that our old friend Jimmy Cook, convenor of the Lothian Regional Council, would approve of our finishing touch. Our drawings showed a new tram line running right up to the stadium. The New Easter Road complex would include a training ground, five-a-side pitches and other sports facilities. It was going to be a seven-day-a-week community sports centre.

Across the city, Wallace Mercer was not going to be left behind. While I worked on Straiton, he suddenly came forward with a plan for a new Hearts stadium. Millerhill was one possibility but Hermiston was also on his radar. The Tynecastle site would be redeveloped to finance a move away in the same way we planned to use Easter Road. The fact that David Murray was involved in the Hermiston scheme only added to the intrigue. If, as Mercer later claimed, his ambition was to smash the Old Firm duopoly, why would Rangers' chairman be helping him? Perhaps the answer was that David Murray had invested in the land at Hermiston and hoped to profit handsomely if the project came to fruition.

The Bank of Scotland, through their managing director Gavin Masterton, had been lined up to back the Hermiston project. David Murray and Gavin Masterton seemed to orchestrate much of what was happening in Scottish football in this period. Masterton had been the man to open up the bank's vaults to the Ibrox club, enabling Rangers to sign the best players in Britain and dominate the league.

The stadium race was well and truly on. On paper, we were in a much stronger position than Hearts. In acreage, the land at Easter Road we owned to fund our move away was more than double that at Tynecastle. Also, while the Hermiston land controlled by Murray lay in the green belt, it formed only a minor part of a vast proposed development of offices and housing. Unlike our plan in Straiton, a football stadium in Hermiston was not attractive to Edinburgh City Council's planning committee. Their convenor, Bob Cairns, memorably described the proposal as "millionaire casuals rampaging through the green belt".

If, however, Edinburgh had only one football club and that club argued that its future existence depended on receiving permission to build a new stadium at Hermiston, the authorities would have come under immense pressure to give their consent. Whether this was ultimately Murray, Masterton and Mercer's plan I can only speculate. What I can say with confidence is that the value of Hermiston, with a football stadium included, would likely be hundreds of millions of pounds to developers.

I was asked in an interview at this time whether I would ground share with Hearts. Straiton was our development, but I did reply that such an idea was a possibility, citing that the sharing of stadiums was common practice in other European leagues. Serie A was the continent's dominant division at the time, and it was striking how many of Italy's big clubs cohabited. Lazio and Roma, AC Milan and Inter, and Juventus and Torino all shared grounds. The San Siro is owned by the city and leased to the clubs. They both have their own separate grand training facilities and club headquarters elsewhere. Perhaps it could have worked for Hearts and Hibs, but I would never consider this if it meant one of the teams disappearing.

I know many Hibs fans did not want to leave Easter Road, and while I understood that sentiment my goal was to restore Hibs permanently to European football's top table. In 1990, Straiton seemed the path to doing that. In retrospect, I think not being more guarded about the Straiton proposal this early in the process was an error. It challenged the status quo and worried Edinburgh's business elite, who jealously guarded their turf. It definitely concerned the traditionalists in Scottish football. My need to disentangle myself and the club from David Rowland's control clouded my judgement. It was a miscalculation that nearly proved fatal.

FOURTEEN

THE BID

ONLY A FEW years ago, I read an article on the damned Hearts–Hibs merger, which asserted: "We will never know what Duff knew about the bid before it happened." So, to put the record straight, here is my answer: Absolutely nothing. Why would I have fought off the bid – at considerable personal expense, both emotional and financial – if I had somehow been 'in' on the plan to destroy the football club I love?

Beyond the throwaway comment of Wallace's wee boy at the school open day, the first I heard of a bid was on Friday, 1 June 1990. It was just a week before the World Cup finals kicked off. I was at my office in Swindon when I took a call from Jeremy James, my fellow board member and Rowland's most faithful lieutenant. "David wants to sell his shares, and he's found a buyer."

My initial reaction was that this could be positive. Hopefully, it was someone who had a genuine interest in football. We could work together and continue to develop plans for Straiton. A new major shareholder didn't necessarily mean the whole managerial structure of the club would change.

My first question was "Who is it?" Jeremy was giving nothing away. The most he would say was that it might prove difficult for me to stay on as chairman. But, he said, if that proved the case, I would receive "a lot of money" for my shares. That was of no interest to me. I did not want to sell Hibs.

Jeremy said that Rowland wanted to meet in London that coming Sunday. When I asked if it was to discuss the deal, he said, "No. It is to do the deal, not talk about it." As there had been no prior discussions with me, I simply did not comprehend what was happening. I pressed Jeremy: "Is it Maxwell?"

"No, worse than that," came Jeremy's amused reply. Without being unkind to Mr Maxwell, I did not think that possible.

I assumed it must be one of Rowland's friends as there was no publicity, no due diligence had been done, and no whisper of a name. Edinburgh is a village of rumours. It still amazes me that the story never got out before the morning of the press conference announcing the bid.

Beginning to worry, I rang Jim Gray. He knew nothing, but he shared my growing concern. I called Sheila. She, too, was none the wiser. There was no alternative other than to travel to London and see Rowland. Jim and I began to 'war game' all the possible scenarios and potential purchasers we could think of. We must have written down a hundred names – the idea that it could be Wallace Mercer didn't cross our minds for a second. Allan Munro – who had joined the board shortly before the acquisition of Avon Inns – agreed to accompany us. He was our business director, and having his early judgement would be valuable if we deemed the proposal to be contrary to the club's best interest.

We were to meet Rowland at his INOCO headquarters next to the London Hilton. When we arrived, the instructions were that I should head alone to his flat, which sat on the top floor of the building. So, leaving a tense Jim and Allan behind, I stepped into the lift and was whisked upwards. Still somewhat mystified by all this stage management, as I entered the room I had no idea what to expect. It came as a surprise to be greeted by only Rowland and Jeremy James. The prospective purchaser was nowhere to be seen. I was offered a seat, and Rowland outlined the basis of the deal, still concealing the buyer's identity. The purchaser, Rowland explained, wanted to be the sole owner of the club and would make a bid at 40 pence a share. This valued Edinburgh Hibernian PLC at circa £6 million net after all debts had been covered. Rowland confirmed that he had already entered into an iron-clad agreement to sell his stake in Hibs, which would trigger a takeover. Put simply, he had done the deal behind my back and there was nothing I could do to stop it.

Looking back, I realise Rowland must have been enjoying keeping me in suspense. The way he signalled for the mystery bidder to enter the room came straight from the pages of a John le Carré novel.

There are moments in life when the brain cannot comprehend what the eyes are seeing. This was one such moment for me. The door handle turned, and into the room strode Wallace Mercer. For sure, I was in shock.

I sat with my mouth gaping open and eyes fixed on Wallace, no longer able to process the English language. Somewhere, I heard mention that Wallace would create a new club, 'Edinburgh United'. Like a concussed boxer slowly coming to, I did manage to ask a few questions. It became painfully clear that Edinburgh United would play next season at Tynecastle Park, wear maroon jerseys and be called Heart of Midlothian. This was no merger. It was the destruction of Hibs for nothing more than money.

Rowland gave me my orders: go back to Edinburgh and appear on stage with Wallace at the press conference scheduled for the following morning, where the deal would be announced. I felt now that I was between the hammer and the anvil. The matter had been settled before it was even discussed. I have absolutely no doubt that if I had agreed to that proposition, Hibernian would not exist as we know the club today. At best, they would be a Scottish Royal Liege, a ghost of a once-glorious past existence.

I was handed the outline of the offer and immediately began thinking about how I could scupper this conspiracy. I knew that we were up against it. The financial institutions would definitely sell. From an accounting point of view, the deal would be attractive to them. There would be no social or emotional consideration. They would take the money and run.

Finally, it dawned on me why Rowland had kept Mercer's bid secret from me until the last possible moment. He knew that I would not go down without a fight.

I raced downstairs to explain to Jim and Allan what had happened. Their faces mirrored the disbelief on my own. Before we could flee the scene of this unfolding crime, we had to endure sitting through an excruciating meal with its perpetrators, including Wallace.

Finally, when Jim, Allan and I escaped, they breathlessly asked me myriad questions. I had no answers. All I could tell them was that there were no circumstances in which I'd be on that stage tomorrow. Instead, we would meet at 9 a.m. at Easter Road and prepare for war.

Several Hibs heroes were born that night. Jim and I were backed unequivocally by our families, even though they knew full well this fight would impact every aspect of their lives. Sheila Rowland confirmed she would not support Mercer's bid, even though going against her former husband would have severe consequences for her personally.

Going into Easter Road on that Monday morning felt bizarre. People were as yet unaware of the impending doom. The staff were their usual happy selves, preparing for an ordinary day at the office. The tsunami would not hit until the press conference was over.

I did not tell Rowland or Mercer that I would no-show their cosy media briefing. I imagined their smug faces momentarily crossed with panic at the realisation I wasn't going to be an accessory to this murder. It was a small but important personal victory; the opening salvo of my fightback.

There was little I could do at this stage until the reaction of the press could be gauged. It felt like being 5-0 down to Rangers at half-time but daring to believe you could turn it around. There was a sliver of hope. Behind the deal was the Bank of Scotland acting at the behest of Masterton. The way the offer was structured, Wallace needed to gain a 75% stake in the club to trigger the bank's funding. It was a possibility that the bank could lower this threshold, but for now, at least, those were the battle lines.

Allan Munro pointed out that we needed stock exchange advisers if we were to oppose the bid. Allan recommended Edinburgh Financial Trust, and our rebel band – which also included the Hibs head of security, Alan Stirling – sought to appoint them at the very time Wallace was laying out his 'vision' to a dumbstruck press corps at the Caledonian Hotel. Their advice was not going to come cheap.

If we were to fight the bid, we needed to somehow convince the Bank of Scotland to hedge its bets by backing the defence as well as the attack. No institution in Edinburgh wanted to be seen as the responsible party in the destruction of Hibernian. The bank was no different, even if Gavin Masterton had agreed to advance the £6 million Wallace required to make Edinburgh United a reality. And so, in keeping with the curious logic of these affairs, with its left hand the Bank of Scotland began lending Edinburgh Hibernian PLC considerable funds to fight off the very bid it was financing with its right. Wallace's original offer had a deadline of 6 July for acceptance. It was to prove a tumultuous five weeks.

Day one was spent entirely in the boardroom at Easter Road. The challenge for me was that I now needed to think solely as a stock exchange chairman rather than as a football fan. Before I could announce that the Hibs board considered the bid to be a hostile one, I had to establish that Edinburgh Hibernian PLC was worth more than Mercer's offer. On the face of it, the offer looked attractive. It was substantially more than the share price. But, of course, this was no ordinary 'corporate takeover'. It was a proposal to asset-strip Hibs and consign the club to oblivion. At the very least, shareholders needed to understand that reality. This may not have concerned the institutions. But it certainly mattered to thousands of fans who had bought shares.

Our first course of action was to search for evidence that would allow us to argue the bid was not in the shareholders' best interest. I kept coming back to the awkward fact that, financially, the offer appeared to be a good one. Wallace and his cohorts valued us at £12 million gross and £6 million net. Ironically, that net worth was far more than Hearts were valued at.

It was clear to me that his next move would be to hijack Straiton. Hermiston looked like a long shot. It would not be the goldmine Hearts hoped for unless Edinburgh became a one-club city with only one potential new stadium. Right from the start, I believed that for those behind Wallace Mercer, this was really about a major land deal rather than creating an Edinburgh team to topple the Old Firm. Murray had his stake in the Hermiston land and he was backed by Gavin Masterton at the Bank of Scotland. My view is that all three men came to see 'Edinburgh United' as an easier path to a lucrative development. The potential profits were vast.

Early on, we did the maths on the ownership of Edinburgh Hibernian PLC shares. The sums made for depressing reading. Following the second share issue, Rowland and the institutions held more than 70%. Mercer was on the brink of having what he needed as Rowland had effectively pledged his shares to Wallace via what is called an irrevocable letter of sale. The institutions would follow suit.

Of the other approximate 30%, I owned 13.5% and the fans roughly 10%. There were a small number of shares, around 4%, that were held anonymously. I came to realise this 4% could swing the whole deal. A coalition of my shares, those of the fans and this anonymous holding would prevent Wallace from reaching the 75% the bank required.

While I have to hold up my hands and accept that by bringing Rowland into Hibs I had left the club vulnerable to this hostile bid, I hope my actions prove that my love of Hibernian is beyond question. I could have accepted an offer for my shares, which would have made me around a million pounds, left the country and allowed the 'merger' to be steamrolled through.

I don't believe Mercer and Rowland ever truly understood football. To them, everything had a price. They assumed I was like them, that ultimately I would be ruled by money. Was I tempted to accept? No, not then; not ever. They were testing my resolve. But I was not going anywhere.

On the day the bid was made public, a crowd immediately began forming outside Easter Road. Accompanying them was a handful of photographers. We drew the blinds on the window to keep the press from getting an uninvited picture. The murky dark of the room reflected our mood. The crowd grew as Hibs fans woke up to the reality of what was happening. The club they loved, that their fathers loved and their grandfathers before them, was fighting for its very existence.

The righteous anger that had been aroused was in danger of boiling over. Menacing graffiti aimed at Wallace was daubed next to the ground, and the window of his Edinburgh office was smashed with a brick. Understandably, it was also the case that some of the fury of those who gathered in front of the stadium was directed at me. Police soon arrived. We invited a delegation of fans inside. We briefed them that while the board couldn't comment publicly on the offer until we'd formally received it, our intention was to fight off the bid tooth and nail. This proved insufficient in soothing the thousand or more fans who had by now assembled.

I know there existed a section of people who thought I had been Mercer's confederate and that it was only fear that drove me to oppose the deal. Let me be as clear as I can in addressing that suggestion. As a Hibee, if I had not been chairman, I would have been at the club's gates with the gathering throng. I was fully aware of the passion of the Hibs fans. Fear never once entered into my thinking.

As the evening drew in, I decided I wanted to go out and speak to the supporters. "That is not possible," was the firm advice I received. I insisted. The crowd needed to know we were on their side, that we were going to fight for Hibs. They needed leadership and hope. A compromise was agreed upon. I would tell the fans that we were legally obliged to entertain the bid but that we were considering all options. I was told under no circumstances should I divulge what I intended to do with my shares as this might prejudice the offer and could result in censure from the stock exchange.

I did not ask for any security guards to accompany me. I went out alone but quickly found myself flanked by the attendant police officers. Rather than a raging mob, those I encountered were frightened. It hurt me deeply to see the pain Wallace Mercer's destructive bid had caused them. I carried with me a chair, which I stood on facing the fans. I started to read from the statement the advisers had prepared for me. I then broke down the maths.

I looked out at the expectant faces and put the paper away. My hands trembled as I locked eyes with as many as possible. I told them what I truly thought of Wallace Mercer's offer. "I will need all your help to beat this," I said, "but rest assured, I will never, ever, sell my shares." I returned to my war cabinet, where I was greeted by the sight of my stock exchange advisers all sat with their heads in their hands.

*

My routine throughout the bid was to get up early and go for a run. I was never confronted, abused or attacked. Alan Stirling had been tasked with keeping Jim and me safe. I was advised to have 24-hour security. I objected. I could tolerate being ushered into cars like an endangered person, but I did not want a security man staying in my house. We agreed that I would be dropped off at night and collected in the morning. From day three onwards, I drove myself. Much was said about how both Wallace's and my own home in Scotland came under threat. I expect it was worse for Wallace, but certainly, at the start, we were both marked as potential targets.

When in Edinburgh, I lived at Cammo on the River Almond. Wallace lived further downstream, on the same water in Barnton. Our houses were in very secure areas, and we were never in any real jeopardy. I based myself in the city for the whole month of the bid. I only left Scotland on Hibs business. Wallace spent a fair chunk of early June in the south of France and watching the World Cup in Italy, so the popular depiction of him being under siege all summer isn't entirely accurate.

The Hibs defence team met every day. The morning was spent at the offices of Edinburgh Financial Trust on Melville Street. The afternoons were dedicated to running the club and continuing to fight the bid from Easter Road. The prospect of the bank lowering its 75% requirement for Wallace terrified me in those early days. This was a glaring area of concern, totally beyond my power.

My chair-top rallying call to the fans made it clear to our advisers that I had the courage of my convictions. Rather than admonishing me, they now understood that this was a campaign I could not countenance losing. By Wednesday, they allowed me to announce that the board had considered the bid hostile. This meant we would not, as a board, accept the terms. I told the Edinburgh *Evening News*: "We have been here for 115 years. We have survived two world wars . . . if you think a bid by local developers is going to stop us you're wrong – Hibs will go on always." Our official advice to shareholders was to reject the offer. Other than Rowland, the one dissenting director was his man, Jeremy James.

We now needed to prepare a defence document showing why we were repudiating the bid. Our logic would have to bear scrutiny from our business-minded institutional shareholders. The defence document would also have to be independently verified. This would take time and needed to be completed away from the public spotlight.

It was natural that Hibs supporters wanted to do all they could to see off Mercer. But we had to balance their passion and desire for immediate action with our need to be legally compliant with stock exchange rules. Some of the more organised fans created a group brilliantly christened 'Hands Off Hibs'. This is a name that will be remembered forever in club folklore.

There is a notion that the management fighting the bid was somehow at odds with 'Hands Off Hibs'. Nothing could be further from the truth. From the very beginning, 'Hands Off Hibs' leaders met with us in the boardroom. We formulated a joint strategy, and they asked us to advise them on how they could make the maximum impact. I remember Kenny McLean

Senior at the first meeting. He was a colossus of a man who would have given anything to save Hibs.

From the outset, the 'Hands Off Hibs' committee wanted to hold a rally. They had several places in mind, including the Queen's Park (home to the annual miners' gala) and Princes Street Gardens. It was the board that suggested it be held at Easter Road. I was happy to hand over the keys to the stadium for this purpose. They did not let anyone down and organised what was to be an incredible event within a matter of days.

"What else can we do?" asked Kenny. This is where 'Hands Off Hibs' implemented the most critical strategy of the campaign to save the club. It has since received the least attention from those writing about the bid.

Such was the ability of the 'Hands Off Hibs' committee to mobilise the club's supporters, they encouraged all Hibs fans with Bank of Scotland accounts to visit their branch and close them. Thousands of fans zealously answered this call. I could not advise this, as the Bank of Scotland was both backing the bid and funding our defence. 'Hands Off Hibs' executed the plan magnificently. The next day outside every branch in Edinburgh, crowds were forming in defence of our club. 'Hands Off Hibs' had advised fans to wear their colours. Each queue looked more like a line for cup final tickets than customers carrying out their banking. Radio Forth, the *Evening News* and even local television loved the story. The passion of the people driven to save Hibernian shone through in every report.

In the late afternoon, the boardroom telephone rang. Jim picked up the receiver. It was Gavin Masterton asking us to call the Hibs fans off. In exchange, he committed to announcing that the bank would not drop the threshold required by Mercer to trigger its funding below 75% under any circumstance. 'Hands Off Hibs' had dealt Mercer a potentially fatal blow. The situation was back under the control of those who loved Hibernian rather than those seeking to destroy it. This was the moment I began to be sure we would win. I slept well that night. Our fortifications were further strengthened by our successful lobbying of the Office of Fair Trading, who referred the bid to the Monopolies and Mergers Commission.

'Hands Off Hibs' campaigners were a constant source of great ideas as we sought to press home our advantage. All Hibs supporters were urged to write to their MPs, and I am sure most did. The rally at Easter Road is the most iconic moment of the fight against Wallace Mercer. It is not for me to recount what happened there, the moving speeches and the outpouring of emotion, only to say that it was the fans' event and the fans' wonderful achievement. My only contribution that day, other than being in attendance, was to give 'Hands Off Hibs' the keys to their home. Several times I left the boardroom and went down to the players' tunnel to watch with tears in my eyes as the Hibernian community united. Many people approached me. No one had a bad word to say. The inspiration we drew from the 'Hands Off Hibs' rally as we prepared our defence document was unquantifiable.

It would be wrong if I did not record here the many others who flocked to the cause of defeating Wallace Mercer. Support for our club ran deep. Both the Lothian Regional Council and Edinburgh City Council immediately threw themselves into the fight. A wise MP, Brian Wilson, sought clarification as to the Bank of Scotland's role in the affair. I would have loved to tell him more. Another parliamentarian, Ron Brown, pressed the matter with the Monopolies and Mergers Commission. John Robertson, the Hearts player, so long 'The Hammer of Hibs', defied his own chairman and became verbally and visibly involved in expressing his disgust at the merger plan. I believe John's brother George is a great Hibee. Children's television presenter John Leslie even wore a specially made 'Hands Off Hibs' T-shirt while hosting Blue Peter.

The fact remained that all these measures would be inconsequential if Wallace got to 75%. Until now, the final blockade that stopped him from reaching his target has remained a secret. It is a profound part of this story that had significant consequences for the direction my life has taken in the years since.

To this day, I believe David Rowland thought he was acting in my best interests by accepting Wallace's offer behind my back. The deal, after all, represented a handsome return on our initial investment in the club. Later on, I think, deep down, he may even have come to admire the fact that Hibs was of more value to me than any amount of money. But at the time such considerations were anathema to businessmen like him. He was a veteran, with the best advisers and brightest minds at his service. In many ways, he had helped frame the structure of the deal to all but guarantee victory. Almost.

If Rowland wasn't going to fight according to Queensberry rules, nor would I. I recounted to my advisers how at the eleventh hour of the flotation miraculous mystery buyers had come to our rescue. Page by page, we began to scour the names of every single shareholder in Edinburgh Hibernian PLC, forensically hunting for those rogue shares.

There were four or five suspect bundles held by offshore banks where the main beneficiaries were hidden. It was now imperative for us to discover who the owners were and whether they were likely to be 'friend or foe' when it came to the offer. I had my own private hunch, but it was no more than that.

We could not force the banks to reveal the identity of the beneficiary. We could, however, ask the Court of Session to disregard those shares from the 75% count needed by Mercer if the beneficiaries failed to come forward. Disenfranchisement would not mean that we now had more shares on our side, but it would push Wallace further away from his target.

This became of enormous importance. So tight were the margins, if this ambiguous 4% holding was taken out of the equation, my shares combined with those of the fans would take us over the finishing line and block the bid. I instructed Dundas and Wilson, the best corporate litigators in Edinburgh. They went to the Court of Session ex-parte (that is without telling or giving notice to the other side) and obtained the Order of Disenfranchisement. The only way these frozen shares could now be counted towards Wallace's target was for the owner to reveal his or her identity. If my suspicions were correct, to do so would cause them far more trouble than it was worth.

The Scottish Football Association represented another potential ally. They did not want to see the demise of a football club that had existed for more than a century. Mercer's bid had been timed impeccably – like an assassination – when we were at our weakest, and the powers of influence in the Scottish game were out of the country preparing for the World Cup.

Jim and I travelled to Genoa, where Scotland were playing Sweden on 16 June. This was a very different World Cup trip than I'd planned just a few months before. Now we were on a rather special mission to talk to the Scottish FA. At a meeting at the national team's temporary World Cup headquarters, we received the assurances we needed. Hibernian's registration would be retained, even if the merger bid went through. Maybe we would play at a refurbished Meadowbank. Perhaps we would even be playing against Meadowbank in the Second Division. If all else failed – a diminishing prospect at this stage in the saga – we would start again in the lowest league. This was purely an insurance policy, the absolute last resort. If Wallace managed to seize our assets, we wanted to make sure that he would never take our soul. There would always be a Hibernian.

Throughout the bid period, I remained in contact with Grant Butchart. He let slip that he had known of Wallace's intentions before they became public. It was a shame he never filled me in. Butchart was the only person I ever met who admitted to any prior knowledge of 'Edinburgh United'. Even today, I wonder whether he had a toe in Mercer's camp. If he did, he never let on. We continued discussing Straiton and ways to keep the project alive.

Around the boardroom table, my team sought to piece together the defence document. In some respects the calculation of the club's assets was straightforward. Andy Irvine, the former Scotland rugby captain and British Lion, who worked as a surveyor, priced up Easter Road. And what we had paid for Avon Inns was a matter of fact. Mercer's bid valued the net worth of Edinburgh Hibernian PLC at close to seven times more than what we had paid for the club three years before. I would later be accused of financial mismanagement, which left the club vulnerable to predatory bids. I can understand this, given that I had failed to oppose the purchase of Avon Inns. But in truth, any listed company, good or bad, can be the subject of a takeover. It was the bankers' decision to back another agenda that precipitated this crisis.

I read, in articles, that supporters were asking how the club could be in so much debt. What they didn't realise was that we had considerably more assets supporting the debt and a healthy net value. Despite the disaster of Avon Inns, my belief is that, in time and left alone, we could have turned things round. Tottenham Hotspur, the only other PLC in British football, had recently included their players as an asset on the balance sheet. I realised that if we did the same, I could prove that Mercer's bid undervalued the club, and I would be able to offer a robust defence against it. The players' registrations were clearly of value. If they had been worthless, there would be no such thing as a football transfer market. To list the players as an asset, our valuation of them needed to be independently verified. The solution was to find an expert who could go through our squad and estimate the transfer value of each player. We turned to the most experienced manager in the Scottish game, Dundee United's Jim McLean.

Jim was delighted to help. He thought the bid was an affront to the decency of football in Scotland, and he clearly had no time for Mr Mercer. Over the years, I believe Jim turned down the manager's job at Tynecastle several times. Up to now, his role has never been fully formally acknowledged in the story, but Jim McLean was another person who played a vital part in saving Hibs.

*

Aside from working on a defence document, one of the first measures recommended by our advisers when the bid was made public was to seek out a 'white knight'. This was a corporate term for the introduction of a friendly alternative purchaser. They told us this was a common tactic in foiling bids of this nature. I would have chosen anyone to buy Hibs above Mercer. We exhausted a shortlist of potential candidates. One name in particular came to dominate discussions. Tom Farmer.

Farmer was, of course, a very successful businessman, having started work as a tyre fitter and progressed to run the largest vehicle exhaust business in the country. Kwik Fit had become a massive company, with its imposing corporate headquarters at Murrayfield on Corstorphine Road. Remarkably, despite its rapid expansion, Farmer still effectively remained in sole charge. We all thought he could be our white knight, particularly as no sooner had Mercer tabled his offer, Farmer let it be known in the local press that as a proud Leither – sensitive to the distress being felt in the community – he was keeping a keen eye on events.

Allan Munro put out the initial feelers. A reply came back that I should meet with Farmer's right-hand man Tom Harrison. Harrison and Farmer had forged an extremely successful partnership developing land and property. At our meeting in London, I set out my vision for Hibs, including the potential move to Straiton and the residential development of Easter Road. Harrison said he would ruminate on this, but told me in the meantime we were welcome to contact him around the clock. Although Harrison had no connection to Hibs or Leith that I was aware of, he, like Farmer, had bought a number of Edinburgh Hibernian PLC shares. In regular statements, issued to the *Evening News* via a spokesman, Farmer was insistent that he had no desire to own the club but instead sought to be a "grey knight" able to have a "powerful voice in the future."

Then as we were compiling our defence document, through Edinburgh Financial Trust I received word that Tom Farmer wanted to meet with me. I was to come to his house, which was close to the Royal Burgess Golf Course, in one of Edinburgh's most prestigious locations.

My team prepared me thoroughly. I knew what questions needed to be asked. But, as an insurance policy to ensure nothing was missed, I wanted Allan Munro to accompany me. Farmer was unequivocal in his response to this request. The invitation was for me and me alone.

I drove to Farmer's house. Next to the grand residence sat a detached outbuilding, which might have once been a stable. I would discover this structure was Farmer's home office. I had never before met this titan of British business and had only seen his black-and-white picture in the newspaper. Upon my arrival, a short, auburn-haired man came out to greet me. He thrust out his hand and introduced himself as Tom Farmer. Rather than taking me to his office, Farmer instead led me to the main house, where we entered through the kitchen door.

Farmer then took me into a comfortable adjoining sitting room, where we sat opposite each other, and he thanked me for coming. After a while, he brought out some ancient-looking parchment which, he explained, contained the minutes of a series of meetings chronicling the rebirth of Hibernian FC in 1891, following a financial crisis for the club. Farmer's grandfather, John, and great uncle, Philip, had both donated £5 to the Hibs cause.

He then dropped a bombshell. "I've brought you here to help you sell your shares to Wallace Mercer." I sat aghast. This was yet another surreal moment when the universe turned upside down. I felt like I was back in that hotel room at the Hilton. Was there no end to the intrigue?

Farmer explained that he had done a provisional deal with Mr Mercer, to buy back the name and memorabilia of the club. He would make sure Hibs survived but would start again from scratch as they had under his ancestors.

The name and memorabilia? I considered this to be all but total surrender. I explained that I was still the chairman of Hibernian. And, as the only person who would be negotiating the club's immediate future, I expected to do much better than that. Farmer returned to the familiar Rowland-Mercer playbook – speaking of the handsome amount of money I would make if I would just check out and walk away quietly.

After the bid, it was said that I was under severe pressure to sell my shares. This was accurate, although it might interest people to know that leverage was being applied from both sides of the Edinburgh business set, 'traditional' and Catholic. The only group who didn't want me to sell were the Hibs fans. Like

Rowland before him, Farmer expected me to accept his advice. That was made abundantly clear by his next suggestion. I should explain at this point that Tom Farmer and Wallace Mercer lived in the same neighbourhood.

Farmer revealed that before my arrival, he had met with Mercer. Moreover, at this very moment, Wallace was on hand waiting to speak with me. Farmer offered to fetch him – I assumed from the stable office – so we could conclude a deal once and for all. He would referee. He also said he would make sure I would be given credit for saving the name and spirit of Hibs. He told me he held great sway among the Scottish press. They, he assured me, would spin the story the way he wanted.

I remember vividly today my first thought. Wallace, next door? What if a Hibs fan walking his dog had seen XX1 and then HIB51 registrations arriving at the house? My relationship with the fans had endured Avon Inns and the bid, up until now, but it was fragile. It would not take much to destroy the trust I had built. I felt I had been put in an impossible position.

"Thank you, Mr Farmer," I said. "I have nothing to say to Wallace Mercer." As I got up and made my way out, I could see by the expression on his face that this was a man accustomed to getting his own way.

*

The defence was now ready to publish and would be printed overnight. When the document hit the stock exchange, those seeking to demolish us saw that just maybe we would win the commercial argument and beat off this wretched bid. There were further twists and turns to come.

Tom Farmer immediately asked to meet again, and we invited him to Easter Road. I may be wrong, but I believe this was only the fourth time the man ever set foot in the stadium. Even though

Farmer had insisted I come alone when we met previously, he brought his company secretary with him to Hibs.

I never once met Tom Farmer without afterwards feeling dumbfounded. We convened in Jim Gray's office, on the ground floor. I hoped he might grudgingly congratulate me on our defence document. Instead, his mood was hostile. "You've done it now!" he said, forcefully banging his copy of the document on the desk. "Wallace might walk away because of this piece of crap." "Yes, Tom, that was rather the idea," I replied. Only later did I come to appreciate that if we fought off Mercer, I might have been able to stay in charge.

Perhaps the most depressing moment of the whole sorry affair came soon after when I saw Farmer again. He was behind an assembly arranged at the Usher Hall in what would prove to be the opposite of the 'Hands Off Hibs' rally at Easter Road. I was invited onto the stage that night. I should have calculated that by sharing a platform with Farmer, I was effectively endorsing his programme. I had fallen into the very same trap that Rowland and Mercer had tried to set for me at that press conference a month before.

The highlight of this evening was an impassioned speech by John Robertson. The Hearts player articulated the view that his chairman did not understand the rivalry between the Edinburgh clubs. He also stressed the redundancies any merger would precipitate. Robertson's rousing finale was to say that he did not want to play for a Hearts that had no Hibs to face.

But this was to be the Tom Farmer Show. He rose to his feet and proceeded to deliver a speech that cast himself as the potential saviour of Hibs and called for drastic changes in the way the club was run.

Now in the final days before the deadline set for the bid to be completed, I received a call from David Murray. The Rangers chairman began bending my ear. He seemed absolutely determined to convince me that it was in my personal interest to sell up.

Murray informed me Mercer wasn't going away. He explained that at the end of the initial five-week period, Wallace would extend the bid by a further seven days. Also, the offer might be increased from 40 pence per share to 45 pence. This, I was told, would give me a legitimate reason to sell, perhaps even a fiduciary duty. Murray seemed fully apprised of the strategies we had used to value the club at a price higher than Wallace's original offer. Those wanting Mercer to succeed knew I had used the innovative accounting procedure of valuing players' contracts.

"Just think about it," Murray said. "You will have that whole week to consider the offer and then walk away with more than a million pounds." £1 million was a lot of money in 1990. It still is.

Others made similar entreaties. I had not spoken to David Rowland since that fateful day in London. Now, suddenly, he asked to meet. I hoped to persuade him to pull out of his deal with Mercer and extract us all from this hell. I flew down to meet him, and a surprisingly gentle Rowland took me to lunch at the famous fish restaurant, Wheeler's. We were both licking our wounds.

He told me that I had hurt him badly by bringing his family and friends into this battle. Some of those shares I'd disenfranchised belonged to his French secretary – the soon-to-be-new Mrs Rowland. Others were held by his neighbour in Monaco. This, he said, had been "the dirtiest of tricks". Maybe so, but this was not a friendly, it was war. The pain he had inflicted on my family would endure for far longer.

Rowland confided that unless I yielded, this would be the first corporate battle he ever lost. And then he uttered some prophetic words that I will never forget: "If you win, no one will thank you for it. You'll be blamed, painted as the villain. It will ruin you, and you'll never work in football again."

Rowland too proposed another way. I could still take the money and be remembered as a Hibs hero. "Throw in the towel. You can say you've done everything within your power to save the club." I've since read reports that Rowland threatened to sue me for frustrating the bid, but I never heard from his lawyers.

Just like Farmer before him, Rowland did not understand my ego. It was ample for sure, but money or manipulated good press would never be worth more to me than Hibs. No matter how often I told these people that, they just didn't seem to understand. They couldn't comprehend football and never would.

Trying to appeal to Rowland – the businessman – I took the opportunity to propose my solution: he could be the owner of Manchester United while helping me to save Hibs. Perhaps fortunately for fans of the Old Trafford club, he was not listening. Depressed, I flew home.

Finally, we reached the deadline. David Murray's prediction that Wallace would extend the window to complete the deal by seven days proved to be spot on. That's exactly what the Hearts chairman did. I could only hope our defence would hold firm. I prepared for the longest week of my life and wondered how the pressure would be applied next.

But nothing happened. The time passed, and nobody called me. The following Friday, I reported to the office of Edinburgh Financial Trust on Melville Street one last time. As we sat in silence, the movement of the hands on the wall clock to 5.31pm signalled the deadline had elapsed. The bid was dead. We drank a glass of wine, and our toast was to Hibs.

Leaving the office, I noticed a top-of-the-range blue Mercedes parked 40 or so yards down the road. As I walked past with Jim Gray, a window rolled down. Sat inside was David Murray. "Well done, you brave bugger," he said, before driving away. Whether he was being genuine or sarcastic, I do not know.

That evening we went to the Hibs Supporters' Association Club. The party was in full swing. The drinks flowed, and the supporters embraced me. This was the last time that I would feel so accepted. After an agonising month, it was the only place I wanted to be. I will never forget that night.

In defeat, Wallace would claim that while he lost the bid, he won the financial argument. There was no financial argument. In the asset-to-debt ratio, Hearts were in worse financial health than Hibs. Had Mercer succeeded, only a move to a new development at Hermiston or Straiton, backed by investors, would have saved his venture. From the outset, 'Edinburgh United' would have been saddled with debts totalling around £13 million; the £6 million owed to the Bank of Scotland for financing the takeover and the existing debts of Heart of Midlothian and Hibernian.

The costs incurred making and fighting the bid, totalling hundreds of thousands of pounds, weakened both clubs. In truth, the Bank of Scotland was the only financial winner. Wallace was, apparently, exhausted by the whole effort, although he later described it as "great fun, a great spoof" which he had "a lot of enjoyment" from. It was a foolish thing to say, and all about his trying to keep face.

I've since heard from fans of school age in 1990 that in the playground, the word was that Hibs and Hearts played a secret match to determine the future of Edinburgh football. The story goes that had Hearts won, Hibs would fold. However, as we triumphed with a last-gasp winner, Hearts were forced to leave us be. Sometimes, I wish we'd been able to settle it that way. I always fancied us against Hearts!

The fight to save Hibs had been won. The battle to own Hibernian was about to begin.

*

That excruciating final week of the bid also turned up one of the most bizarre and darkly humorous episodes of my time in Scottish football. It concerned the departure of John Collins from Easter Road.

Selling John was not something I wanted to do. The three-year contract he had agreed to sign – one of my first acts as chairman – was up, and he was ready to move on. Bill McMurdo believed it was time to progress his client's career, and John took Bill's advice.

John had told us his intentions before heading off to the World Cup. Nothing that transpired over the summer was an influence on a decision he had already made. Of his options, John wanted to go to Celtic, who were very keen to have him. Negotiations were cordial, and they met our valuation of £1 million. John was to be Celtic's first million-pound player. Bill was happy with the personal terms offered to John, and the whole deal was ready to complete.

On the morning that John was to attend Parkhead for his medical, he came and thanked us. He was always a thoroughly decent man. Shortly after saying our goodbyes, word reached us in the boardroom that Rangers wanted to hijack the deal. They were offering to utterly eclipse both the fee agreed with Celtic and the personal terms on offer to John. I was staggered. How could I ignore this? We called Bill on his car phone. He was on the M8 with John sitting next to him in the passenger seat. Bill and John pulled into the services at Harthill, and we discussed the unexpected development.

Rangers had never been on John's radar. However, we were not surprised that they wanted a potentially world-class player. By now, I fully understood their intention was always to get one over on their Glasgow rivals. Rangers had pulled off the ultimate coup the previous summer when Mo Johnston had sensationally snubbed a return to the Bhoys and joined them. This had made Mo the first high-profile Catholic to play for the Ibrox club.

We agreed that John and Bill should continue on to Parkhead. John could have his medical and then discuss the unexpected turn of events with his folks. One suggestion was that he delay making his final choice until the next morning, postponing the formal contract signing with Celtic until then.

However, there was to be no persuading Rangers that John should be allowed more time to reach a decision. I was left in no doubt that it was now or never. The deal had to be done on 12 July and that day alone.

In these weeks, I had been stunned more than once. This just about topped the lot. Ultimately, I believe John's father settled the matter by making it clear to his son that if he went to Ibrox he'd be disowned! John completed his transfer to Parkhead, where he became a true Celtic great.

FIFTEEN

A KWIK FIT

LIKE MOST HIBS fans, I had mixed emotions ahead of the first derby game of the new season after everything that had happened around the bid. In a way, it felt like a cause for celebration that a fixture between Edinburgh's two great clubs was taking place at all. But the bitterness harboured by our fans towards Wallace Mercer was palpable, and it erupted when Hearts took an early lead. Pat McGinlay was the unlucky scorer, unwittingly diverting John Robertson's speculative cross past Andy Goram. Hearts fans from behind the goal spilled onto the pitch and were met by some angry Hibees, one of whom completely lost his head and went for Robertson. That was very unfortunate as Robertson was the Hearts player who had spoken out so courageously against 'Edinburgh United'. Thankfully, Goram intercepted the irate fan and the police managed to restore a modicum of order.

Soon after the game restarted, further trouble broke out. Referee Jim McCluskey took the players off the pitch. After a lengthy delay, play resumed again, and Craig Levein added a second with a header from a corner. Then, with half-time just a minute away, Hearts made it three through John bloody Robertson – who else? John has since recounted that during the interval, the police match controller came in and pleaded with the Hearts players not to score any further goals for fear of sparking more violence! The match finished 3-0 to Hearts. In the end, I believe there were 46 arrests made that afternoon, with 17 fans suffering minor injuries. It was an ugly day in Edinburgh's footballing history. All this had been unleashed by that toxic, hostile bid. Having initially vowed to be "first off the team bus", Wallace was advised to stay away from the game by the police. Fortunately, he had the good sense to listen. I dread to think how much worse things would have been if he had not.

In the weeks before that dark occasion, I had already succumbed to those demanding I resign the chairmanship. Tom Farmer had been one of the loudest of the voices calling for me to go.

David Rowland remained the major shareholder but seemed more determined than ever to remove himself from the club. Tom Farmer, who readily admitted he was no fan of football and had insisted that he had no desire to own the club, became the dominant presence.

With Rowland's blessing, I remained on the PLC's board. I was driven by my desire to continue with the Straiton project for the benefit of Hibs. In retrospect, I recognise this was a mistake. I should definitely have walked away completely.

Back in 1988, David Rowland had wanted to float the Hibernian Football Club Limited, a company more than 100 years old. Thankfully, I had insisted we form a parent company, Edinburgh Hibernian PLC, ensuring the football club was ring-fenced. In resigning the chairmanship, I agreed to a compromise that would see Jim stay on the football club board. At the behest of Farmer, Alistair Dow was installed as chairman of the PLC. I am sure Alistair was a good corporate man, but he had no background in football or feel for running a club. He would call me nearly every day, asking for advice.

Along with Dow, the new PLC board included Allan

Munro, Tom Farmer, Tom Harrison, Jeremy James and Jim Gray. Rowland added Derek Moran, a really sharp corporate accountant, and me. At our first board meeting, where we sat unable to find a consensus while debating how to move forward, Derek turned to Farmer and asked his opinion. The legendary reply came back: "See you, you've all got your fancy degrees and education. I'm just a simple tyre fitter." Behind this persona lay a ferociously ambitious man.

Ahead of the PLC's Annual General Meeting in early 1991, a motion was tabled calling for a vote to have me removed altogether. Rowland made it known that he would oppose such a move, and with the institutions giving Rowland their vote by proxy, I survived. Frustrated by the stasis in the boardroom, Farmer instructed his accountants, Arthur Andersen, to undertake a business appraisal on the board's behalf. But they never once asked for my input, and it seemed to me they were working solely to Farmer's interests.

Consequently, I decided I would have to organise a resistance. My best chance was getting back to Grant Butchart and progressing Straiton. The proposed development was exciting and worth tens of millions of pounds, which represented a game-changing fortune for the club. Since we'd just escaped oblivion, I reasoned that surely the planners would want to help Hibs. Nevertheless, there came a time when I realised that Grant Butchart was engaged in detailed discussions with Tom Farmer. When I challenged him, his response was to ask, as long as Hibs benefitted from Straiton, did it matter to me who delivered the deal? My answer to this is the same today as it was then. If Hibs were the beneficiaries, it did not matter at all.

And then, on the Monday following the final Edinburgh derby of the 1990/91 season in March, the *Edinburgh Evening News* published what I felt was a character assassination of both Jim Gray and me. Neither the paper nor the journalists who wrote the article, David Forsyth and Jim Baillie, had approached me for comment before publication. In my opinion, the piece was deliberately timed to undermine me and sabotage my work at the club. What's more, it was personally devastating.

The article attempted to portray me as a bon vivant, flying all over the world on Hibs' money. I've recounted in the preceding pages the trips I made in service of the club, and I accept that my legal practice required me to travel frequently between London and Edinburgh. But anyone who has taken the air shuttle will attest there is little glamour involved in that particular journey! The article went on to criticise our hospitality, salaries, cars and even our use of mobile telephones. The Serious Fraud Office's investigation into Les Marston was also highlighted. It was now impossible for me to challenge Tom Farmer. I could see that my credibility was shot.

*

Before I was finally ousted from Hibernian, Tom Farmer asked me to meet him at Kwik Fit's offices in Murrayfield. Sitting in the reception, I flicked through the only reading material on offer: several beautifully bound testimonials praising Farmer and his business. It struck me that perhaps visitors were deliberately kept waiting to ensure this result.

Farmer's appetite for 'doing business' was voracious; he was never satisfied, always looking for the next opportunity. There was much to admire about the man. He was incredibly successful and really did start out as a tyre fitter. All his achievements, which were far, far greater than my own, were the result of his hard graft, flair for salesmanship and single mindedness.

Having collected me from the waiting area, Farmer took me over the road to a high-end restaurant. He said nothing in particular beyond throwing out the odd cliché about the importance of "trusting each other." He was clearly assessing me and determining whether I posed any threat.

I mentioned our past meetings and how he had desired that I lose the corporate fight. Farmer was determined to downplay this. As he explained it, all he had done was to offer to set up a summit between Mercer and me, which I had chosen to decline. No harm. No foul. I smiled back at him. I would be too ashamed now to disclose what I was really thinking as he spoke. Farmer also smiled. He then sent me on my way with these parting words, "You're just a big teddy bear, son."

A few days later, Grant Butchart came to see me. It was now his definite assessment that our best chance of delivering Straiton was to join forces with Farmer. I said I would back this only on the condition that Farmer confirmed he was progressing the deal to the benefit of Hibs.

Owing to the boardroom deadlock, Edinburgh Hibernian PLC – by now renamed Forth Investments – fell into receivership. As the biggest creditor, the Bank of Scotland was in charge of what happened next. The bank appointed Arthur Andersen as the receiver and they oversaw the uncoupling of Easter Road from the football club. With Kwik Fit being one of Arthur Andersen's biggest corporate clients in the UK, other parties potentially interested in taking Hibernian forward complained bitterly of a blatant conflict of interest. Despite a £4 million offer from a consortium led by former chairman Kenny Waugh – which vowed to keep Easter Road in Hibernian's possession – and interest from two lifelong Hibee businessmen in the Borders, Farmer was allowed to purchase the club and the best of its assets for a reported bond of £250,000. Under these new arrangements, the football club was to be owned in trust, with supporters who had bought a stake in Edinburgh Hibernian PLC receiving shares. Separately to this, the stadium and the club's surrounding land now belonged to a new company called HFC Holdings. Farmer owned a 90% stake in this entity.

The acceptance of the Farmer plan saw the end of my time at Easter Road. Soon after my departure, Hibs travelled to Hampden on a wet Wednesday night to play Rangers in the 1991 League Cup semi-final. In truth, it was a painful experience for me to see Hibs under Farmer in with a chance of winning silverware. The fan inside me was thrilled at the prospect of a first major trophy since 1972. But I feared victory would cement the new regime's control of the club, which I believed could only be damaging. Ironically, Andy Goram proved decisive in sending Hibs through to the final. Having signed for Rangers that summer, he was experiencing a rough start to his Ibrox career, making mistakes in a series of big games. With half an hour played in the first half, Andy came sprinting from his goal to punch a lofted ball clear of the onrushing Mark McGraw. His intervention only served to deliver the ball to the feet of wee Mickey Weir. Mickey looked up, before chipping the most exquisite pass over the stranded goalie for Keith Wright to head home the game's only goal.

Andy subsequently told me the story of the stick he received from his Rangers teammates. Apparently, at training, after Hibs had gone on and won the final, he made the mistake of saying "If I was still at Hibs, I'd have a League Cup medal in my pocket." Without missing a beat, Ally McCoist fired back, "If you were still at Hibs, then we'd all have League Cup medals in our pockets."

I didn't receive a formal invitation to the final against Dunfermline. Instead, I travelled up incognito from Blackpool, where I had taken my family on holiday. I entered Hampden as a paying customer with a friend. Watching them play on that great occasion, I reflected that so many of the players in the team were boys that had begun to flourish during my time at the club. It confirmed to me that we had been on the brink of achieving something truly special. Mickey Weir was the outstanding performer as Hibs ran out 2-0 winners. One of Scotland's top football writers, a big Hibee, told me how the next day he woke up early and rushed to the newsagents. He wanted to send the back page commemorating Hibs' first trophy in nearly 20 years to some of his relatives in America. When he explained the contents of his envelope to the post office clerk, the postie said, "You're the third one already this morning who's done that." I understood the intensity of that sentiment, and later the emotional outpouring at the victory parade along Edinburgh's magnificent Princes Street. After all, it was only just over a year earlier that these same fans had feared for their club's very existence.

Unfortunately, however, rather than heralding a golden new era for Hibs, the League Cup win proved a false dawn. Farmer, Harrison and Butchart pushed ahead with a Straiton project that appeared broadly similar to that I'd hoped to deliver. Significantly, though, under the new agreement they'd struck, their nascent consortium Straiton Ltd – and the land it controlled – had not entered into a profit sharing partnership with Hibernian. I must stress here they were absolutely entitled to do this. Hibs never owned any land at Straiton. But it wasn't the plan I'd be working on with Butchart, which I felt could transform the club into contenders.

Applications for a new football stadium on a 50-acre plot and a commercial development on an adjacent 80-acre site were quickly submitted. Straiton Ltd's stadium build was to be financed by a combination of the commercial revenues the development would generate, grants from the football authorities and money from the European Community. They announced the stadium would be gifted to the community, providing Hibs access to a new modern ground.

I believe the initial spec for the 'New Easter Road' at Straiton submitted to the planning authorities was for a 25,000 all-seater ground based on Anderlecht's Constant Vanden Stock Stadium.

Poor Dougie Cromb – a thoroughly decent and devoted Hibs man who became chairman after Farmer's takeover – was dispatched to sell this vision to fans. With the August 1994 all-seater stadiums deadline approaching, the club's official line was that remaining in Leith was "impossible". Cromb promised fans "Straiton is for us – it will be a Hibernian stadium. There will be a lot of heart-rending leaving Easter Road but the fans and players deserve better facilities." However, having seen their hopes of lobbying for permission for additional commercial development on the 50-acre stadium site quickly frustrated, Straiton Ltd zoned in on an alternative way of making this all add up. The *Sunday Times* reported that Farmer's partner Harrison had jetted out to the South of France for talks with Wallace Mercer. With the Football Trust offering a £4 million handout to clubs willing to build shared stadiums, Hearts were invited to join Hibs at Straiton. Mercer steadfastly rejected these overtures. And so, in late 1994, came a handbrake turn from Hibs.

Despite earlier briefings that there was no way of staying at Easter Road, the club announced its intention to redevelop its existing home while Straiton Ltd's commercial development of Straiton on their 80-acre site soon began apace. Those running Hibs signalled they had listened to the fans and that the move had been "laid to rest". Watching how all this had played out from the sidelines it occurred to me, for now, at least, football no longer served a purpose for those controlling Straiton. Nevertheless, a few weeks later, the Hibs board discreetly informed the planning authorities that permission for a Straiton stadium would remain "very useful" because "football clubs' circumstances could change very quickly and dramatically".

Hibs did get their new home. It was their old home at Easter Road. A home they no longer owned. In fact, they would now have to pay rent to the Farmer-owned HFC Holdings for the privilege of using their own ground. Supporters were even asked to put their hands in their pockets and donate £100 each to help fund works on the stadium.

As the 1990s progressed and the Old Firm galloped away irreversibly from the rest of Scottish football, it seemed the quality of the team on the park was no longer top priority. Thousands of fans resolved to demand the disinterested Farmer place his "Hands On Hibs" or sell the club to someone who would. But even when supporters brandishing water bombs interrupted the gala reception Farmer hosted on the Royal Yacht Britannia, berthed in Leith docks, he refused to budge. By then, Sir Tom had been knighted by both the Queen and the Pope.

Contrastingly, Hibs' fortunes were downwardly mobile. I recognise some will argue that this was the price of financial stability given all that had transpired. Having finished second from bottom in 1996/97, at the end of the 1997/98 season, the club was condemned to Scottish football's second tier – relegated for only the third time since it had joined the elite ranks more than a century before. Perhaps moving to mollify discontented fans and discourage further dissent, it was announced later that year that Easter Road Stadium would be sold back to the football club.

The answer as to why Farmer rebuffed those potentially interested in buying him out of the club may lie in what was happening in Edinburgh's East End. Labour's landslide General Election victory in May 1997 came with the promise of a devolution referendum. Scotland voted to restore its own parliament. In 1998, Holyrood was chosen as its location. With it came a demand for more well-placed accommodation in the city. In January 1999, *Scotland on Sunday* ran an article under the headline: "Hibs Owner Farmer Wants Hearts Merger". The newspaper reported several meetings held between Farmer and Edinburgh art dealer Glenn Ross at Kwik Fit's Headquarters. There, according to the article, Farmer told Ross that "Wallace was right, but he just went about it the wrong way"; furthermore, he explained he had commissioned a study that showed Edinburgh could not support two football clubs. Following these revelations, Farmer issued a denial. Subsequently, however, Simon Pia, author of the original article, was contacted by another source who disclosed he too had met with Farmer and had heard him make similar statements championing a merger.

A year later, Tom Farmer and Tom Harrison's company, Morston Assets Limited, unveiled plans for a £35 million housing and office development of the Lochend Butterfly. This would incorporate 12 acres of land controlled by the council and the plot beyond Easter Road's East Stand, previously owned by the football club, that now belonged to Farmer's HFC Holdings. Just as with Straiton a few years before, Hibs were useful in polishing up the proposal. If Morston Assets won the bid for the Lochend Butterfly, part of the deal would see the increasingly decrepit East Stand at Easter Road rebuilt, complete with an "international class" sports, fitness and medical centre.

Despite the seeming strategic advantage of already owning part of the land required for the development, Farmer and Harrison's bid for the Lochend Butterfly failed. According to *The Herald*, Morston Assets offered £2.5 million plus 35% of any extra value added to the land in the future, whereas Morrison Developments' winning offer to the council was for £12 million. Subsequently, Farmer called for an inquiry into this decision and argued that the land should be put up for sale again. Intriguingly, at this juncture, the plan of a shared Hibs and Hearts stadium at Straiton was resuscitated.

Both football clubs had accrued vast debts in rebuilding Easter Road and Tynecastle. By December of 2002, Hibs' debt was reported to be touching £17 million. Whether the reintroduction of Straiton by Farmer was genuine or a mechanism to apply leverage on the council to reopen the tender for the Lochend Butterfly, I can only speculate. It may also be significant that in 2003, the authorities re-zoned Easter Road from light industrial to residential. In the end, once Farmer had exhausted all avenues to reverse the Lochend Butterfly decision, meaning definitively that the acres of land beyond the East Stand separated from the club had failed to unlock the prized development, it was time for HFC Holdings to cash it in. The *Evening News* put this divestment at around £10 million. But the newspaper cautioned fans against hoping the windfall would be spent on the team given the club's debts and those of its parent company.

Despite planning permission originally being granted ten years before in 1999, the club finally announced its intention to rebuild the East Stand a matter of weeks before permission for the build lapsed. When the stand reopened in August 2010, it had taken fifteen years to rebuild Easter Road. In that time, star players like Kevin Thomson, Steven Whittaker and Scott Brown, were sold off to Rangers and Celtic for millions. For a second time on Farmer's watch, the club were relegated in 2014.

*

There was little I could do when these events began to unfold at the start of the 1990s. I was out of my depth. If I spoke out in opposition, it would cast me against the perceived saviour of Hibs. Who was going to listen? I was a spent force. And anyhow, by then, I had my own personal fight to contend with.

My life took a drastically different direction, and nothing would be the same again. Those around me who I loved suffered, and they still suffer today. I often reflect on Rowland's warning that I would be blamed and ruined. Had I been able to foresee how this would all play out, I might have done things differently. But I cannot absolve myself of responsibility. I played my part. My actions unintentionally allowed the club to become vulnerable. Of course, I have my regrets. I take some comfort, however, in knowing that by refusing to sell my shares to Wallace Mercer, I did all I could to save Hibernian Football Club.

EPILOGUE

NEARLY EVERY ARTICLE written about me over the last 30 years ends with the line, "David Duff received a two-year prison sentence in 1993 for matters unconnected with Hibs." Nothing in our journey through life is unconnected; all events link to each other.

The timing of Forsyth and Baillie's broadside about me in the *Evening News* could not have been worse. I sometimes wonder if it was the article that prompted the Serious Fraud Office to look further into my affairs. They had developed a bit of a reputation for long-winded investigations that delivered few results. A high-profile conviction would go some way to justifying their vast expense to the public. The newspaper's lurid front page must have seemed just the hook they needed.

Although shaken by what had happened at Hibs, my personal future away from football was still optimistic. My property business and legal practice were in good shape in London and Swindon. I did have sizeable mortgages and bank loans. But these were all manageable against the income the properties yielded.

This changed when the banks and other lenders received notices from the SFO, asking for documentation and revealing that I was under investigation. One by one, my loans were called in and properties repossessed. Some of my friends and family were too scared to support me or disclose that the SFO had approached them.

The Serious Fraud Office went through every aspect of my life with endless hours of questioning. Eventually, I was charged with committing mortgage fraud. The SFO also pointed the finger at my assistants in London and Swindon. Was this their punishment for remaining fiercely loyal and refusing to extricate themselves from suspicion by condemning me?

It was brutal. My finances were complicated, and foolishly I had allowed myself to be sucked into the Thatcherite dream of endless wealth creation. I did secure multiple mortgages by presenting my income to lenders in a way that allowed loans to be approved. I was naive and emulated what seemed to be a common practice among my yuppie associates. I was not blameless. I made mistakes and I have paid the price many times over. I have also served my time. Many others have not.

By the time I started my sentence in Ford Open Prison, I was so exhausted that it probably saved my life. In all, I spent a year at Ford, where I ran the charity shop and recuperated from the beating I felt I had taken from Edinburgh's business heavyweights and the SFO. Jail was not a terrible experience. But even in an open prison, where inmates 'enjoy' a degree of freedom, I can say hand on heart the best day I had inside was far worse than the worst day I had as a free man. Partway through my sentence Les Marston arrived at Ford. We kept our distance.

My family home was repossessed. We had to start again from scratch. The matter would dictate the rest of my life. I will carry the stigma with me until my dying day. Nothing now will dissuade me from the belief that if I had sold my Hibs shares to Wallace Mercer, none of this personal devastation would have happened.

I am not motivated to write this book in revenge. My purpose is simply to show how a critical part of the Hibs story has been lost. Dismissing me as a fraudster and disgrace – citing matters that bear no relation to my chairmanship of the club – diverts attention away from the events I have tried to describe in these pages.

This book has attempted to set the record straight by revealing what really happened all those years ago. Of course, it is only my view. It is, however, an informed view. I was involved at every turn, every twist.

One of the first things I did to get back on my feet after leaving prison in July 1994 was to take a lease on a sports ground. I called it the Western Green Country Club. My friend, Tom Douglas, from Lambourne, kept faith with me. He scoured the papers and found two old sports clubs owned by the General Electric Company, and we secured them both on lease without a premium. After a year of hard graft, cultivating the grass and refurbishing the sports facilities, I negotiated a partnership with Premier League football club Wimbledon, who used the pitches for their youth and women's teams. My contribution to their club was recognised in their match-day programme, which meant a lot to me. A top non-league side also came to use the pitch too.

It did not take long after my release for Grant Butchart to contact me with an offer of help going forward. While I might hope that he felt regret at how things had transpired, the stark warning he gave me when we met in Chelsea to watch myself suggested his concern was that what I knew might sabotage his ongoing Straiton development with Farmer, which was at a sensitive point.

I did get to know one of Butchart's children, who wanted to share in a nightclub project I was working on. Later I was told that Grant Butchart sold his share in Straiton Ltd for £17 million.

Many years ago, I told my story to the respected Scottish journalist, Simon Pia. Our relationship started when he – not unreasonably given what followed – questioned David Rowland's motives for investing in Hibs and the wisdom of my plan for flotation. While I may have disagreed with some of what he wrote then, it was evident that he loved the club just like I did. After I left Hibs, Simon and I watched several games together, and I began laying out to him what had happened at Easter Road and Straiton. Simon went away and began to publish in *The Scotsman*. However, following a series of articles that gave voice to concerns about Farmer's stewardship of the club, Simon was gagged. It is worth noting that Kwik Fit was one of the biggest advertisers in the Scottish press.

*

For better or worse, I am part of Hibs' history. In 2024, I returned to Easter Road for the first time since the events I have relayed here took place. I was kindly invited to the reception for the late great Peter Cormack by his wife Marion. I was heartened to be warmly received by old friends, ex-players and fans. I had spent the previous 33 years only occasionally able to watch Hibs when they visited Parkhead, where my son had become a season ticket holder. On those occasions surrounded by the Celtic faithful, I always had this sharp sense that I was sitting in the wrong end. I would feel overcome with sorrow as I lamented what might have been. But I have never stopped cherishing my shirts and Hibs memorabilia, which I am giving to the Hibernian Historical Trust now that I have had the chance to tell my story. At last, after so many long years, I can again feel at one with the club I love.

In closing, I want to reflect on what happened to my Hibs heroes. I have always maintained that I never considered selling my shares to Wallace Mercer. But had I not had the unconditional support of my family, I cannot say honestly that this would have been the case. They are my personal heroes.

Sheila Rowland defied her former husband in resisting the bid. I hope the fences between them have since been mended. Sheila is a Hibs Hero.

Kenny McLean Senior and Junior were inspirational in organising and leading 'Hands Off Hibs'. They recognised early on the sense in working with the board. Kenny Senior has since passed away, but I give my thanks and respect to these two Hibs Heroes.

Jim McLean, manager of Dundee United, stuck his neck out and assisted us in an ingenious piece of accounting that properly valued the players' worth to the club. I was saddened to hear the news of his death while I was writing this book. Few men have left such a mark on Scottish football.

John Robertson was the Hearts player who scored against Hibs over and over again, but when his boss schemed to make Edinburgh a one-club city, he stood shoulder-to-shoulder with those fighting to save Hibernian. Whether he wants to be or not, he is a Hibs Hero.

Another Jambo, Jimmy Cook, got the city fighting Mercer, as did other politicians. Jimmy died an old and wise man.

Allan Munro may have led me to Tom Farmer, but I believe his work in seeing off Edinburgh United remains worthy of recognition.

Jim Gray stayed on for the 1990/91 season, continuing to give his best for the club in extremely challenging conditions, until the powers that be dispensed with him. He was a talented and dedicated football administrator and was instrumental in my Hibernian dream. Jim is retired now. While it has been too painful for us to speak about Hibs in the years since we left, we remain friends.

Then there are those who I feel metaphorically occupied the away dressing room in my story:

David Rowland did come back to football finance via his company Fordham Sports Management Limited. Among other things, the company acquired the image rights of Manchester City's top stars. It was this kind of deal-making that interested Rowland in the game. Very briefly, he was announced as the Conservative Party treasurer. He lost that position due in part to the protests of Hibs fans.

David Murray never built a new stadium on his land in Hermiston, nor did he acquire Manchester United. Many years later, he sold Rangers for £1. Not long after, the Ibrox club spectacularly crashed.

Gavin Masterton left the Bank of Scotland in 2001 and bought Dunfermline Athletic Football Club. According to *The Scotsman*, a controversial £12 million loan from the bank to Masterton's company East End Park Ltd – secured against the club's stadium at the height of the 2008 financial crisis – eventually had to be almost entirely written off. Dunfermline entered into administration in 2013. Gavin Masterton was declared personally bankrupt in 2014.

Grant Butchart sold his shares in Straiton Limited and relocated overseas.

Tom Harrison confounded his 'star businessman' billing when the company he built, Norfolk House, went into receivership in 1991. His partnership with Tom Farmer in myriad property firms proved far more enduring.

Wallace Mercer passed away at the relatively young age of 59 in January 2006. I find it sad that his footballing legacy will be that he was the man who tried to destroy Hibs. I believe he was just a part of a bigger game. I have no ill feelings towards him personally. 'Edinburgh United' was just plain wrong.

And that leaves Sir Tom Farmer, who died in May 2025. His

legacy will be as the man who saved Hibs. His time at the club finally came to an end in 2019, when he relinquished control to Ron Gordon. There is much about his 28 year reign at Easter Road I do not understand. There are so many questions I suspect will never be answered.

During correspondence before the publication of this book, Sir Tom denied ever meeting me at his house in 1990, urging me to sell my shares or doing a provisional deal with Mercer. It is curious, therefore, that Mercer told journalist Ray Hepburn of a meeting he had with Farmer at a restaurant in the quay at Leith before the bid was made public. According to Mercer's account of this dinner summit, as told to Hepburn, Farmer produced two small squares of paper and asked Mercer to write down what he was willing to spend on the takeover of Hibernian. Mercer penned a seven-figure sum and passed it across the table. Farmer had agreed to do the same, sliding his paper over to Mercer. Written on it was £0.

If Hibs fans want to hail Tom Farmer the club's saviour then so be it.

For me, there are far more worthy heroes, humble heroes. They wear green and white to Easter Road every other Saturday.

ACKNOWLEDGEMENTS

DAVID DUFF

I had no idea when agreeing to an interview with football writer Ewan Flynn that he would inspire me to finally write this book.

As we sat in the Curve Garden in Dalston, Ewan's journalistic skills unlocked memories of events I had long suppressed. So started a collaboration which saw Ewan ploughing through my tangled prose, checking, testing and recrafting what I had written.

Ewan turned my story into a publishable book. His patience with me and advice have been of immeasurable help. I could not have wished for a better partner in this project. One of the most touching moments of the writing process came when I told Ewan I no longer had a copy of 'Hibs Heroes'. Within a few days, he had procured the record in its green sleeve for me.

This book has also led to another reunion of sorts. While, since leaving Easter Road, Jim Gray and I have always remained friends, his reading of this manuscript has – at last – afforded us a chance to better understand the damage done to both of us by the way events unfolded. Just as importantly, it has enabled us to relive some treasured footballing memories that we shared together.

I'm indebted to journalist Simon Pia for hearing me out in the 1990s and for being kind enough to write a foreword to this book.

I thank Alan Pattullo of *The Scotsman*, who read an early draft of the manuscript and has been resolute in his enthusiasm for the project ever since. Further thanks go to Luke Shanley at Sky Sports. Luke provided me with videos of matches I had not seen in decades and copies of the defence documents that ultimately saw off the Mercer bid.

Some of the people who were crucial to my Hibs dream all those years ago have now passed away. This book is a testament to the late Alan Stirling, who acted with the utmost professionalism and care as our security officer. Cecil Graham, our indefatigable club secretary. And John Kerr, the young solicitor who shared in my vision for Hibs, and did all he could to make it come true. My mother and father were also a constant source of support, and this is their story too.

It may be over thirty years since my time at Easter Road. But I will always be a Hibernian soldier.

EWAN FLYNN

I would like to thank David Duff for letting me help him tell his extraordinary story. I know it has been painful for him to relive much of it. His candour and patience in answering the thousands of questions I have fired at him during the writing of this book shines through on every page. Thanks to Hugh Andrew, Andrew Simmons, Deborah Warner and Peter Burns at Arena Sport for believing this was a story that Edinburgh football fans and the Scottish game needed to hear. I'd like to say a massive thank you to Hibee Sean Allan. Sean has been a brilliant sounding board and is a repository of knowledge on all things Hibernian FC. Ian Colquhoun and Bobby Sinnet, two excellent chroniclers of the club, have both been unwavering with their help too. Simon Pia, Alan Pattullo, Colin Leslie and Ray Hepburn are journalists whose work I greatly admire. Without their support, this book would never have made it to publication. Thanks to football finance expert Kieran Maguire for his generosity in answering my questions. Finally, thanks to Esther, my partner, for her wisdom and kindness. Hail! Hail!

INDEX